CW01666139

Ben Hartley Notebooks

PIGS MUST EAT ON SUNDAYS

Other publications on Ben Hartley

Ben Hartley
by Bernard Samuels
A survey of the paintings
Published by Sansom & Company

Ben Somewhen
Limited edition of a set of 104 ink drawings
Published by Bernard Samuels in aid of UNICEF

Ben Hartley Notebooks

PIGS MUST EAT ON SUNDAYS

Introduction by Bernard Samuels

Green Books

First published in 2005
by Green Books Ltd
Foxhole, Dartington
Totnes, Devon TQ9 6EB
edit@greenbooks.co.uk
www.greenbooks.co.uk

Text and images © Bernard Samuels 2005

www.ben-hartley.co.uk

Designed by Peter Campbell

Printed by HSW Print, Tonypandy, Wales, UK

All rights reserved. No part of this publication may
be reproduced, stored in a retrieval system or transmitted
in any form or by any means - electronic, mechanical,
photocopying, recording or otherwise – without
the prior consent of the publishers.

British Library Cataloguing in Publication Data
A catalogue record for this book is available
from the British Library

ISBN 1 903998 68 9

INTRODUCTION

Ben Hartley kept notebooks all his life. As a child, growing up in Mellor on the edge of the Peak District, living next to his grandparents' farm, he made scrap-books. At the start of his student days he began drawing in small pocket notebooks, a practice which carried on through the years at art school in Manchester, then in London, at the Royal College of Art, on through to his final years in Wales, in the Border Marches.

It was realized quite early on that he had a gift for drawing, a great consolation given that he was a sickly child, confined indoors for much of the time. The proximity of his grandparents' farm was a great boon. This provided opportunities to get to know farm life, and the memories of those times became the bedrock of his creativity; they remained with him to the very end.

At the time of his death in March 1996, at the early age of 62, there were some 320 notebooks, all of which he left to me. In addition there were 900 paintings, all in gouache, usually on brown parcel paper, now becoming known for their humour and Ben Hartley's gift as a colourist.

I had known Ben Hartley since 1976 in my capacity as director of Plymouth Arts Centre. At the time of our first meeting he had been teaching part-time at Plymouth College of Art since 1960. His former colleagues and students remember him with great affection and respect for his work.

News of the bequest of his work arrived completely without warning. In 1983 he had left Devon and the village of Ermington in the South Hams where he moved the year after he came to Plymouth. He had moved to live in Presteigne, a small town on the Welsh side of the Border Marches. Soon after arriving there he made a will leaving all his work to me. Typically, he never made any mention of this in his lifetime. On balance, I think I am happier that he chose to make his extraordinary gift in this way.

Since receiving the bequest I have organized many exhibitions of his work. In 2001 I brought out a monograph, entitled simply 'Ben Hartley'. It provides an overview of the work, concentrating on the paintings, using the notebooks only in so far as they refer directly to the paintings. But the notebooks have, as it were, a life of their own. In his student days he filled them with observational drawings. Though known to many for his reticence, he had a great love of words and a passion for poetry. All this begins to come through in the notebooks when he settled in Devon and, for a time, words become as prominent as drawings. The notebooks become a record of country life as he finds it in his immediate environs, coloured by the attachment nurtured by his childhood experience.

Seeing notebooks is always a fascinating experience. Living with notebooks, as I have these last eight years, is a very special experience, not easy to put into words. It is an incomparable way of coming to know an artist, a direct way in and something to be treasured. At the same time, how does one share this experience?

By their nature, notebooks are always a problem. There is a limit to the extent you can allow them to be handled. You can show them behind glass in display cases, a page at a time. They can be copied onto CD-Rom or shown on video; but they are, of course, books on paper, not electronic images. I have therefore decided, as a way in to solving the problem, to bring out this small publication and have chosen to home in on just two years from Ben Hartley's earlier days in Devon, 1964 and 1965.

The period is covered in seven notebooks, all similar in shape and size. I have made a compilation from these seven notebooks, reproducing all the material I have chosen facsimile. I hope it gives a sense of Ben Hartley's personality, his mood and his way of life at the time. This followed a regular pattern: teaching in term time, in vacation time visits to his parents in Mellor, near Stockport, and his older sister Monica and her family in Shobdon, on the Herefordshire side of the Border Marches, where they had moved in 1958.

Frail as he was, Ben Hartley travelled a good deal during his vacations. In the summer of 1964 he visited Yorkshire, making an especially charming record of towns, villages and great church buildings in the East Riding. The same pattern continues into 1965, but then takes a most surprising turn in the summer with a visit to Norfolk. After a preliminary visit he abandons his teaching at Plymouth College of Art to join a project called the Church Art Project in the parish of North Repps, on the south side of Cromer.

As usual, we have very little information as to what led up to this somewhat dramatic episode and its equally abrupt conclusion. On the other hand what we do have is a particularly beautiful notebook from the three months spent at the rectory in North Repps with the family of the then Reverend, later Canon, David Ainsworth. A few years later it becomes apparent from the notebooks that the episode in Norfolk was a stage in Ben Hartley's conversion to Roman Catholicism in the autumn of 1968. In the meantime he keeps the lead-up to this major event in his life well in the background. At North Repps we simply find Ben Hartley at his most poetic, in his depiction of life in the parish and especially in his touching impressions of the rector's two small daughters: just a few lines, a touch of colour and a few very simple words.

I hope this book conveys a fraction of the pleasure I have derived from this remarkable bequest.

Bernard Samuels

1964

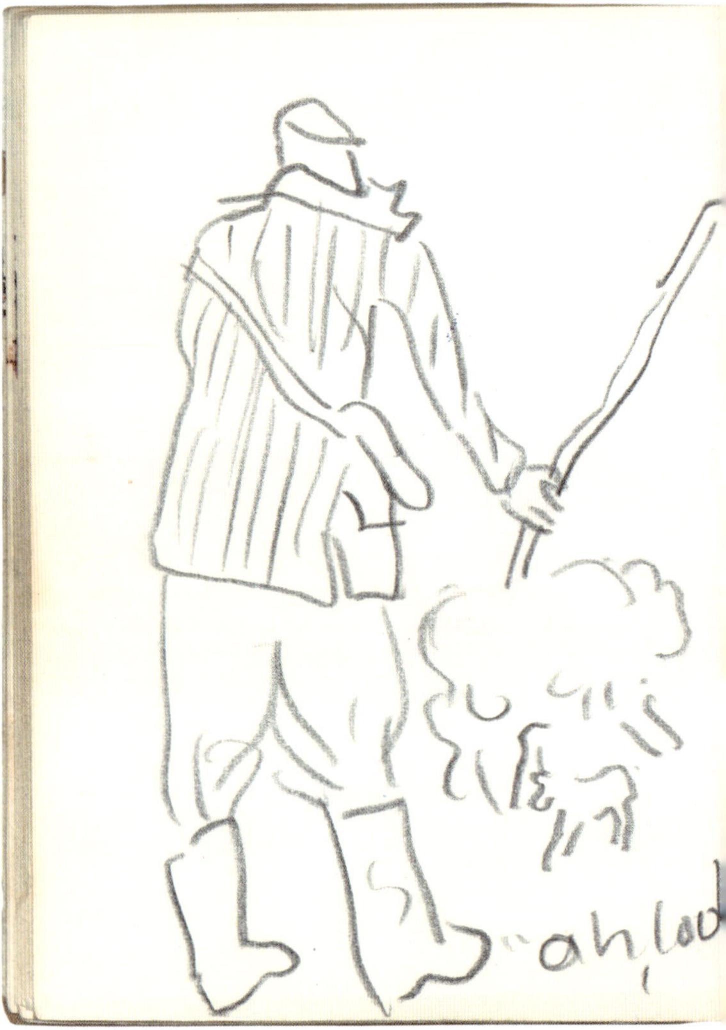

"ah, lad

4th Feb

A Frost - soon gone

Marmalade cooling
in a window

Lambstails

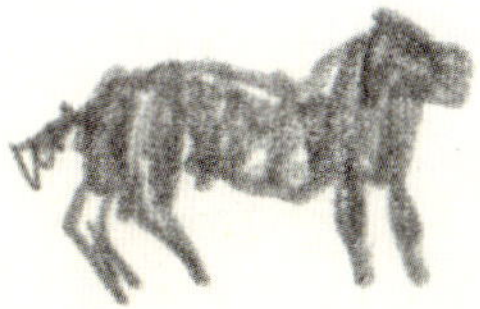

A Sound of spring
marbles - rattling in
a boy's pocket

The first picking
of nettles - tingling fingers!

The River in the moonlight
like a thousand silver fish

monday 24th

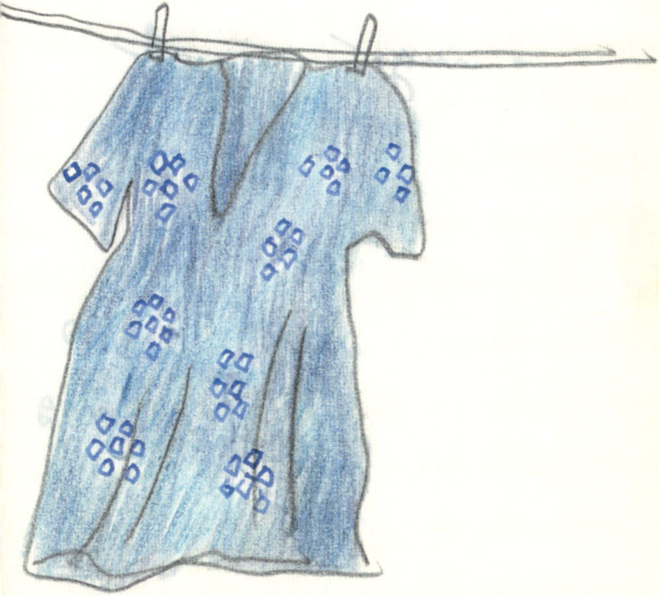

A "Granny" Frock

Read the List of Rectors
& the history of the font

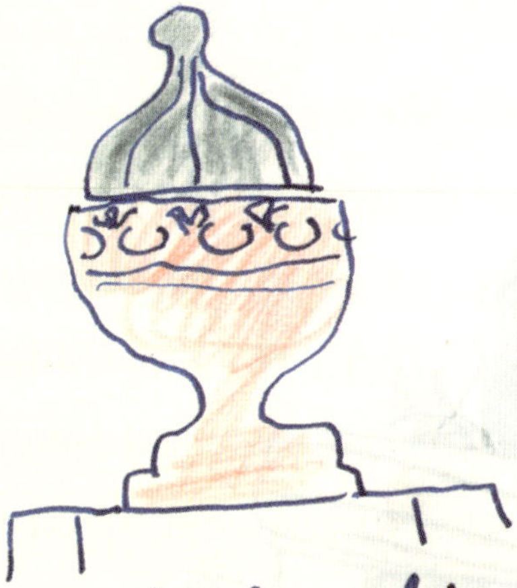

Counted the chimes —
& waited for them
almost counted the prayer
books
The hassocks are comfortable
The bus — a blessing

26 Feb.

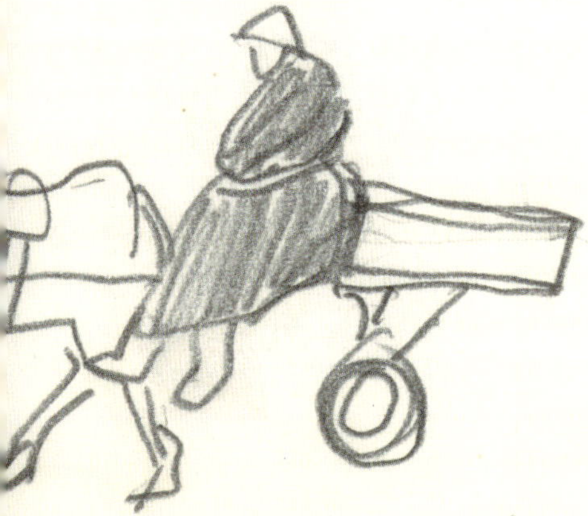

in the wet

4th

as cold &
as grey – today
as yesterday

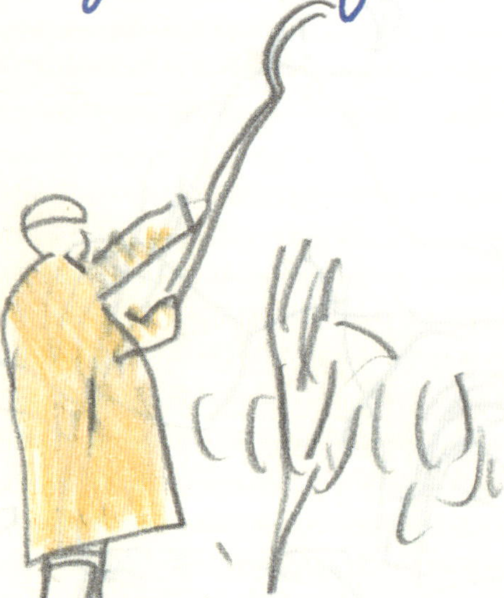

Gardening begining

5th

Still attacking his hedge
(Mr S.)
The slaughterer –
still slashing

Cold, dry, grey & songless.

7th

Cold & Easterly Wind
still blowing

22nd Cuckoo
Woods of garlic-smell &
swallows silver breasted

Blue-skied day
skimming along
skipping, thrilling
wind-blown breath-in-deeply da

Been a boy again:
trespassed ...
& scrambled earthy banks
& almost had ta cross a
stream upon a fallen tre

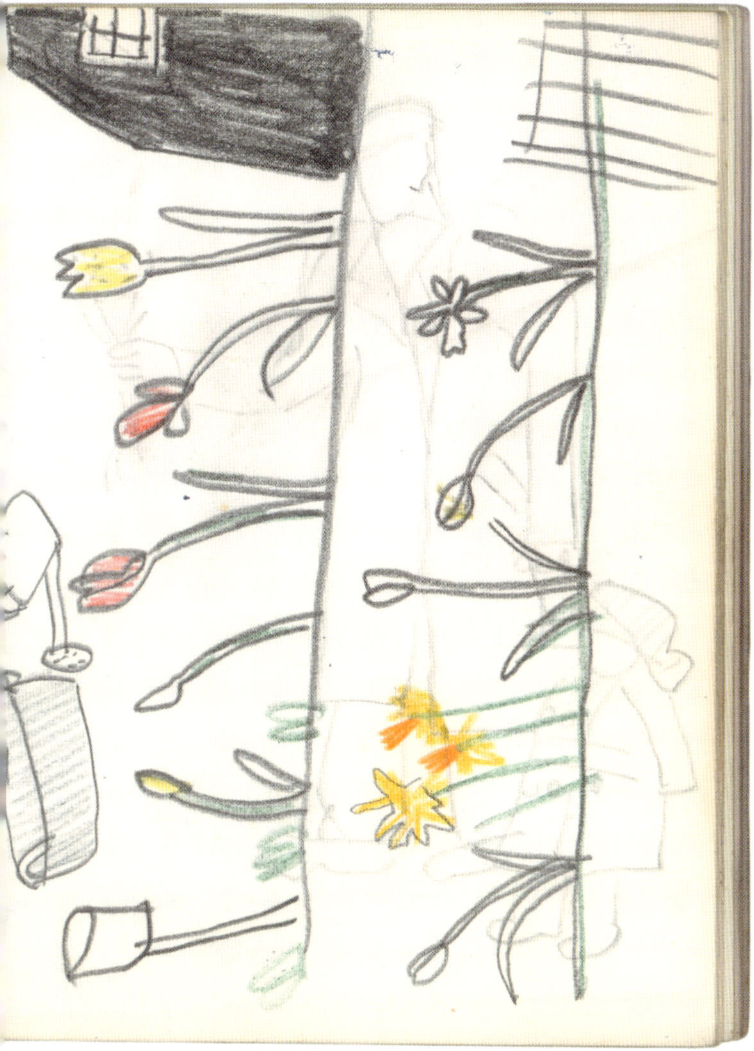

29th

armadas of milk bottles
at The Creamery - Daws.
& why go to London?
why? — The world is
so green..

a horse chestnut
in full dress

On Paddington station:— I spy
folk 'grown-in-gardens'
country feet & the
herbaceous-border-look
of the Un-londoners

11.50 To Penzance

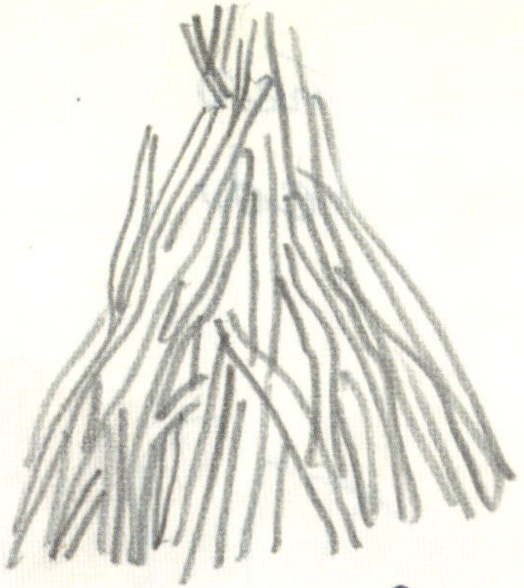

Fish & chips & champagne

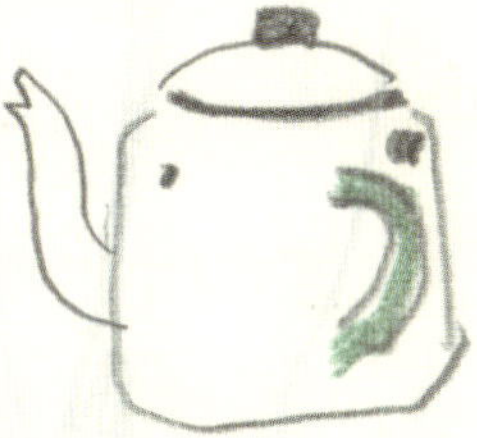

Tin-teapotted-Tea Newbury

16th

Heat & travelling ......

Waiting (Totnes) reading

– with a bag of bluebells

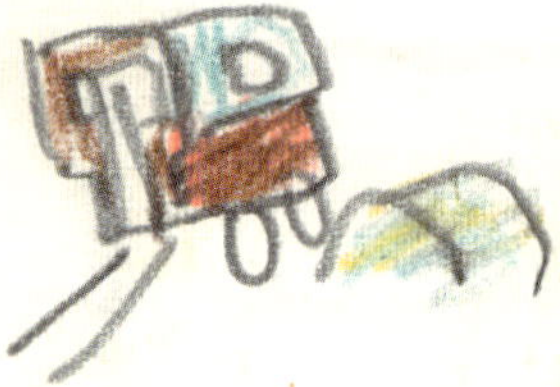

"Get me Virginia Water"

Pontrilas, Pontrilas –
green, Green, Golden Valley
Herefordshire. Heavenly
views

Tram Inn,
sun out
– & hot

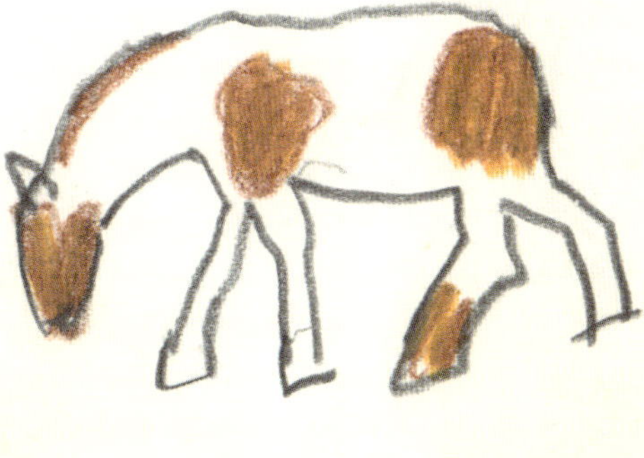

Happy Herefordshire

16 May

That look – that smell –
that smoke ......
& the grim greyness
The brick boredom
The shallow sky

a week at Mellor

19 May

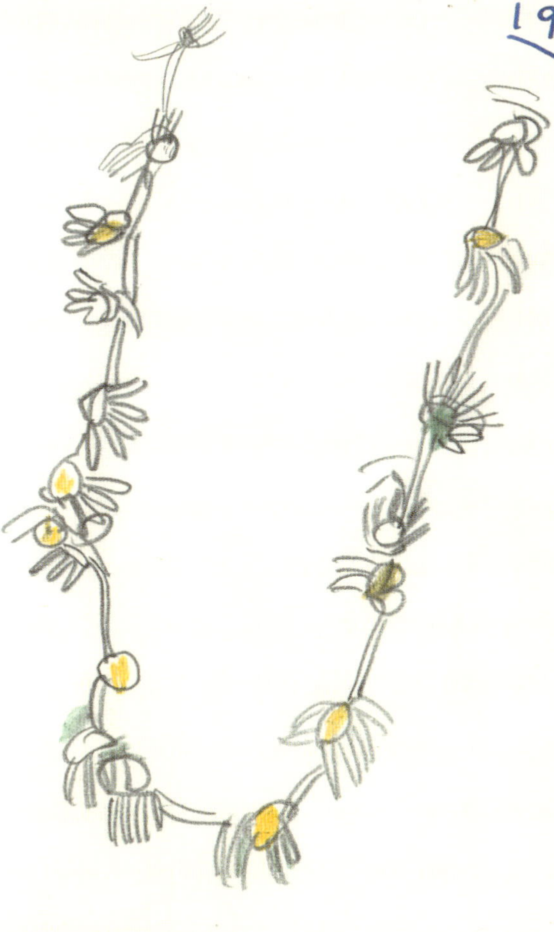

24th

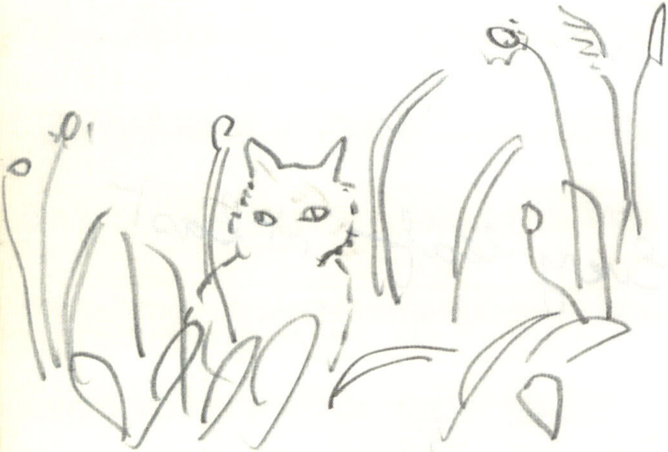

choir boys run,
— I amble

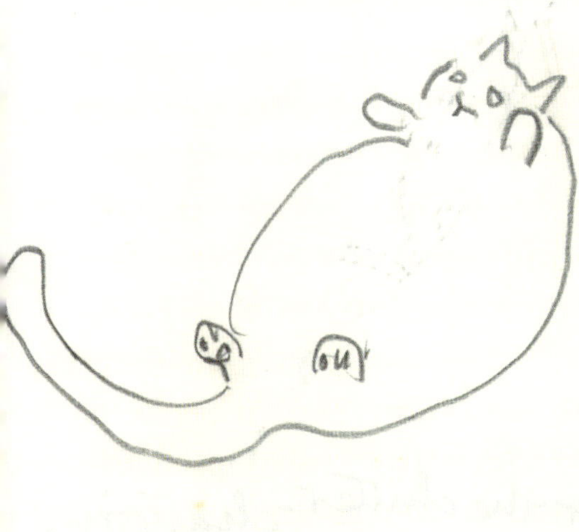

28th May

Waiting, waiting
for the Sweep

29th

a golden evening
& the light is from Heaven

30th may

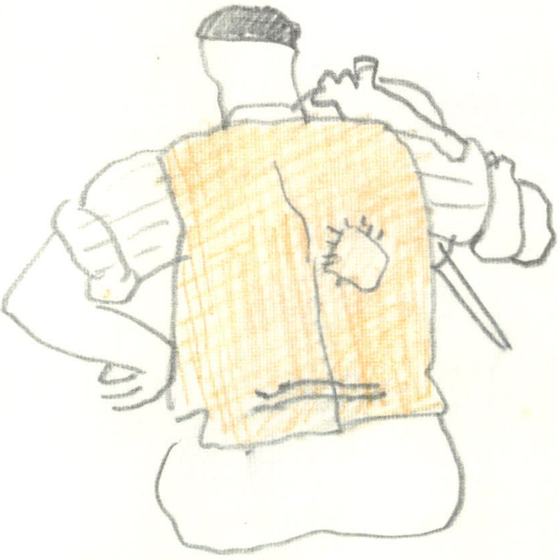

five ravens! Flete
& cuckoo-company

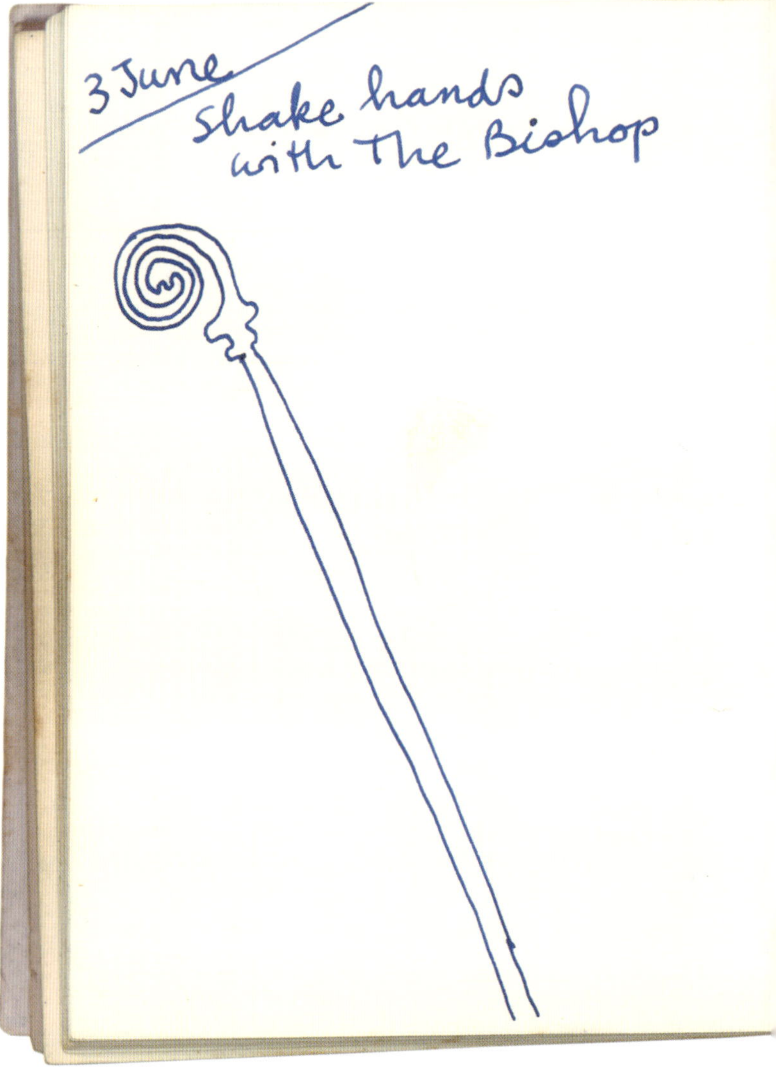
3 June
Shake hands
with the Bishop

They are cutting the grass...

the hedges are summer-high

4 June

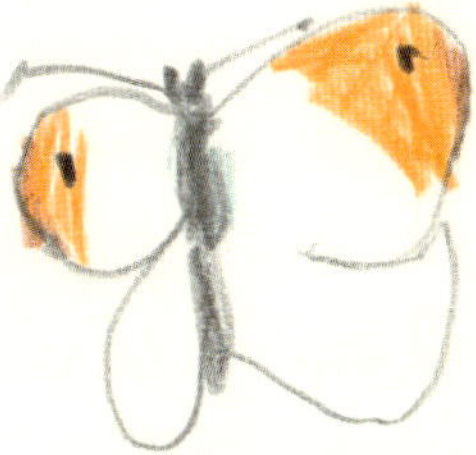

Summer-lush
hedge-high
& flower-bright
the lanes

6th

a slug, duck & snailday
– darkest & rainiest
& strawberries from the hedge

Trinity II June 7th
Rain, Rain on the roof

The collection
rolls on the floor
The churwarden is in
time
'are you making hay?'
'well, we're thinking
about it.'

8th June

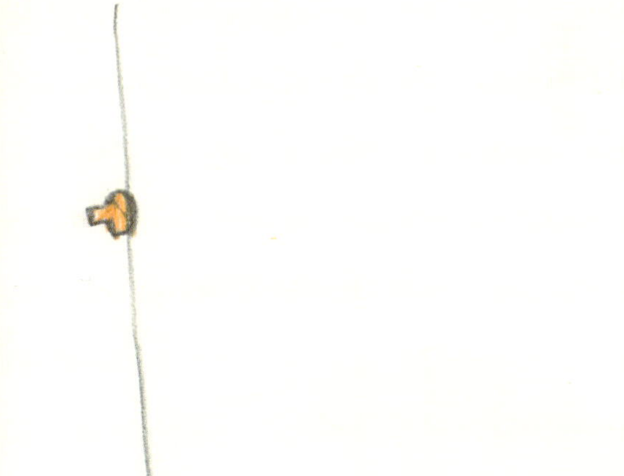

a deaf dog barking –
ambs as big as their dams

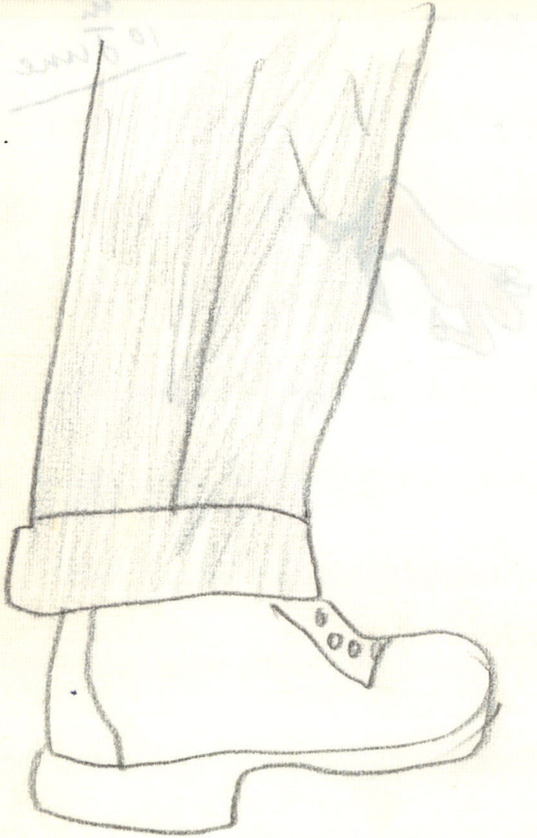

Kings Arms Kingsbridge

11th June

a bag of sticks.
A Mission Service -
minus-Many
The calves are at the back
- over the wall - Friesian maps
of black & white archipelagos
& islands eating grass.

12th

Wet for the Mission
- so my second-best hat.

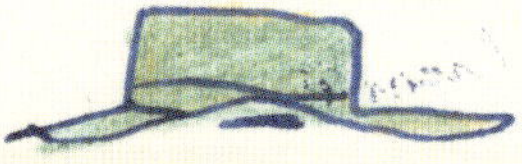

a grandmama's "bun"

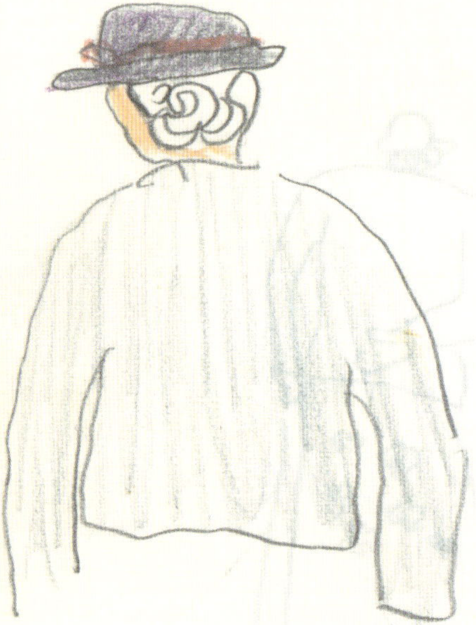

cracks in the ground &
– a hole in my shoe
& this is summer

Barnowling, Linhaying

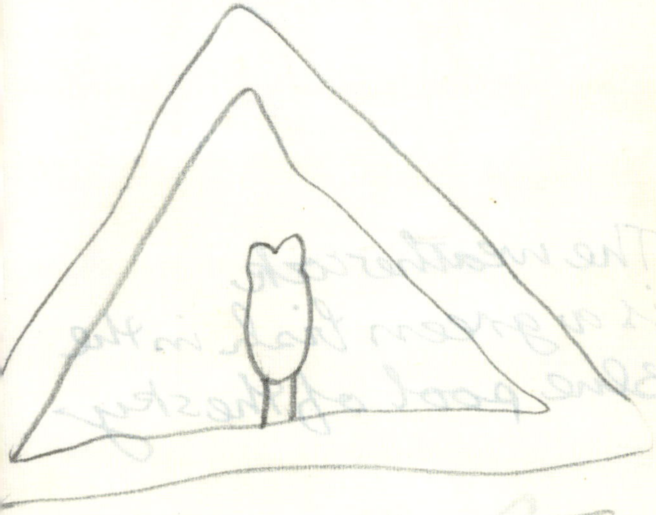

12th July

Trinity VII

Thistletide
& ham & egg for dinner

Little wren - a farthing of a bird

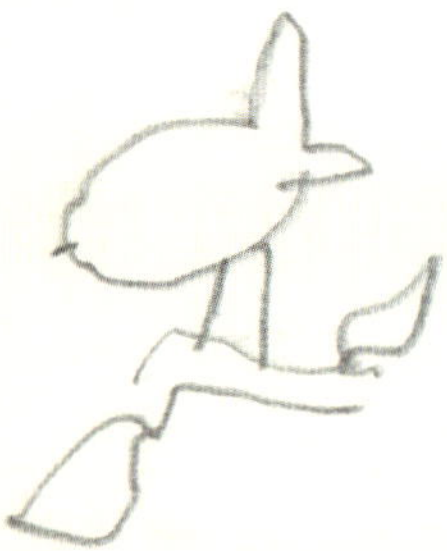

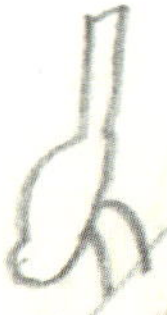

Sunday village -
Sunday quiet
Pram-pushers
& after Chapellers.

13th July

a grey day
a pale day
– pale as rinsing water
Mondayishy
wishy-washy

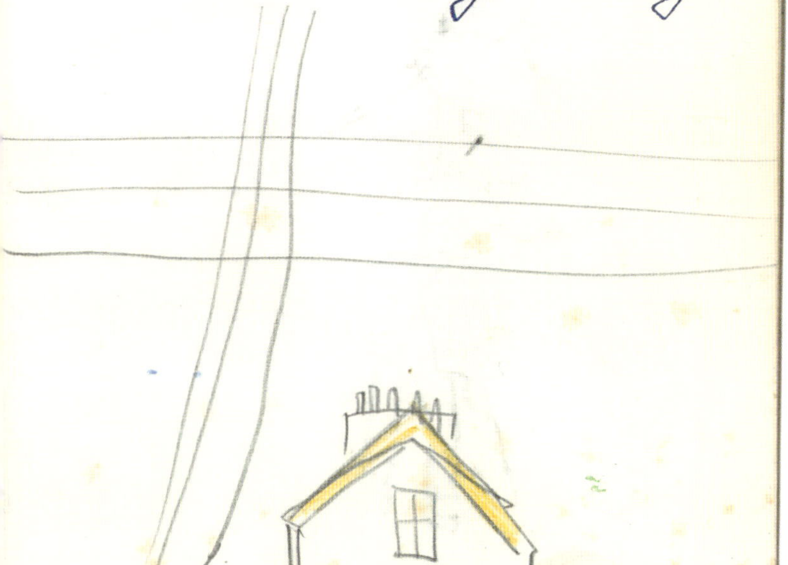

16th July

Bright with Butterflies

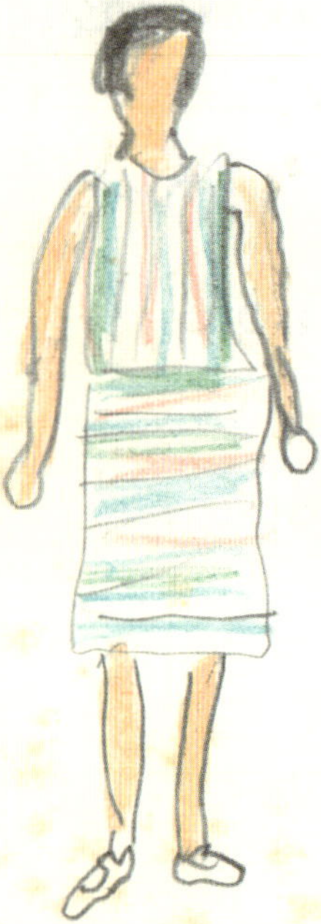

The silence of a Summer day
but not unhummed by insects

Crockers Cleaning
Bonfire-to-be

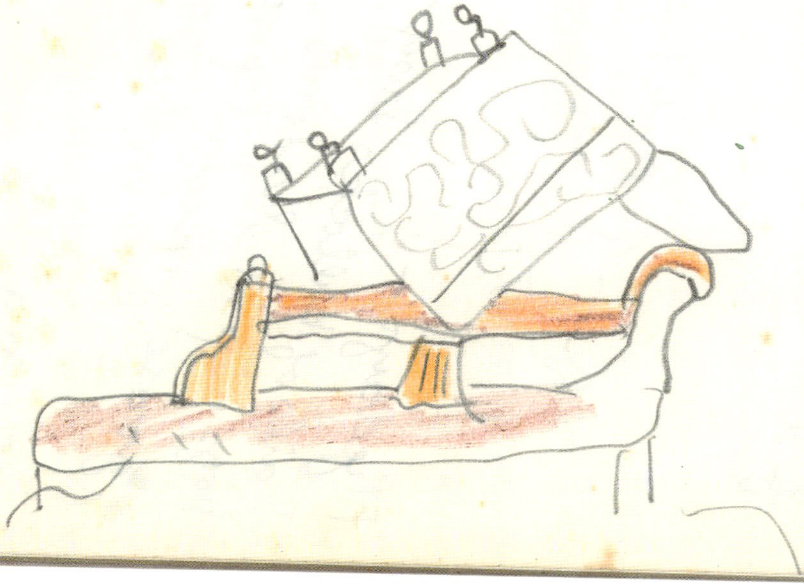

rusty alarm clock
of a pheasant

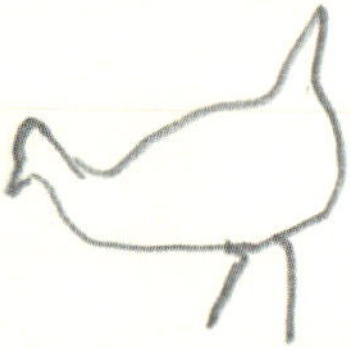

perky trotting
moorhen

Flydays —
Tails of bullocks busy.
Dogs nap in shadows
& a goose: graceful procession
in the road

such a sky
- mottled white

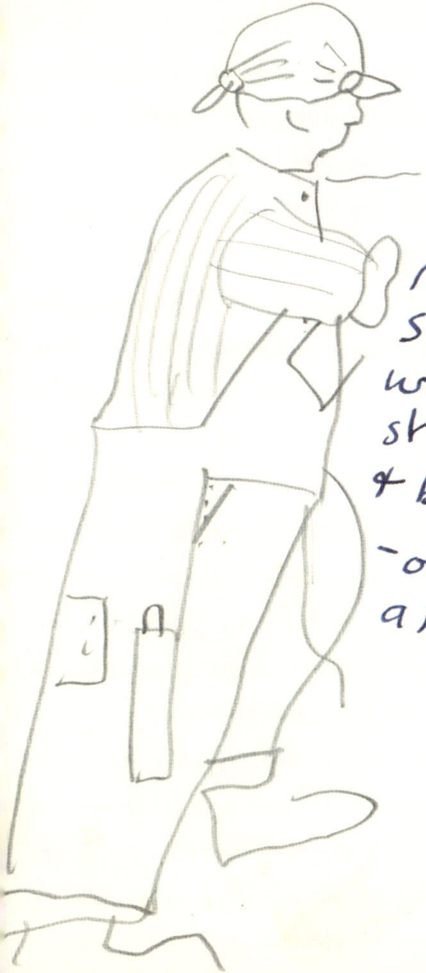

16th July

Met his spaniel
Springer type
with worn teeth
studded collar
& brown patches
- old as
a horsehair sofa

19th

Sunday snoozing-time
The afternoon time quiet
Of paper-reading-slumbers.
Don't disturb the people having
naps

Poor bullocks' faces
devilled with the flies
the

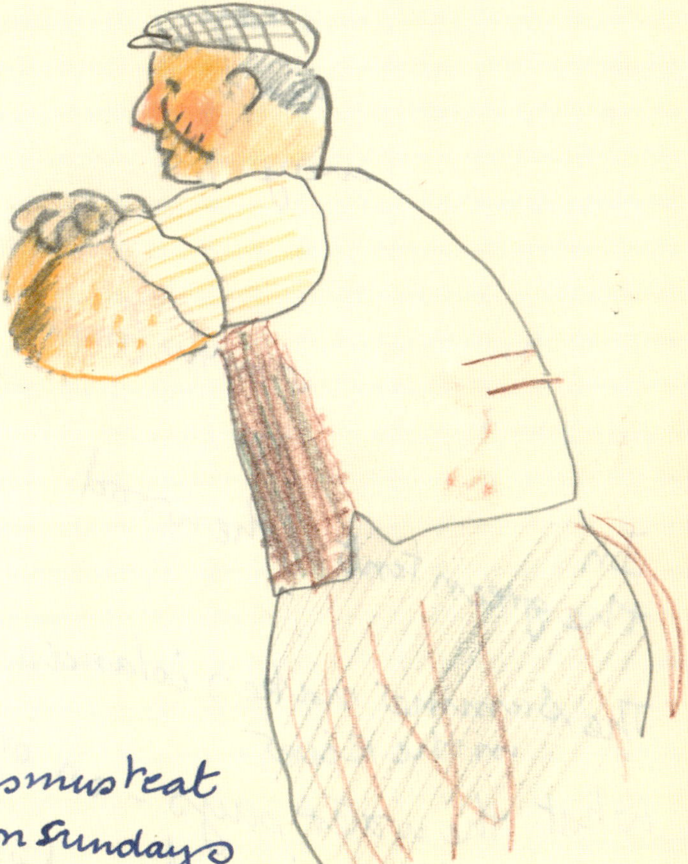

Pigs must eat
on Sundays

22nd / To Plymouth, to the bank

The heat is waving & the
distances are not there...
The heat is wavering over –
over the South Hams

honey colour cows, –
evening-gilded.
What day is it? Soon
I will have to notch a stick.

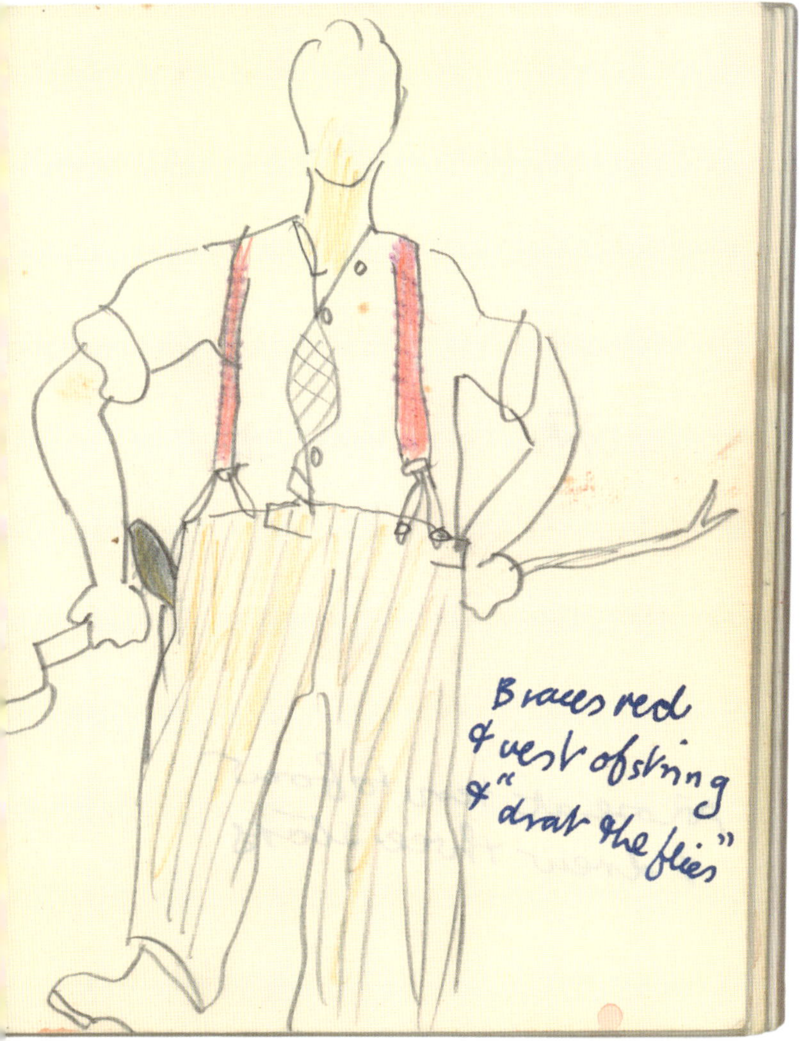
Braces red
& vest of string
& "drat the flies"

23rd July

ARose at ten to four
& drew three stars

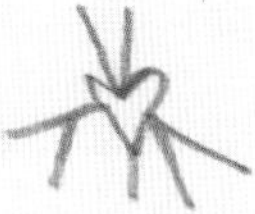

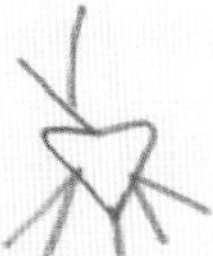

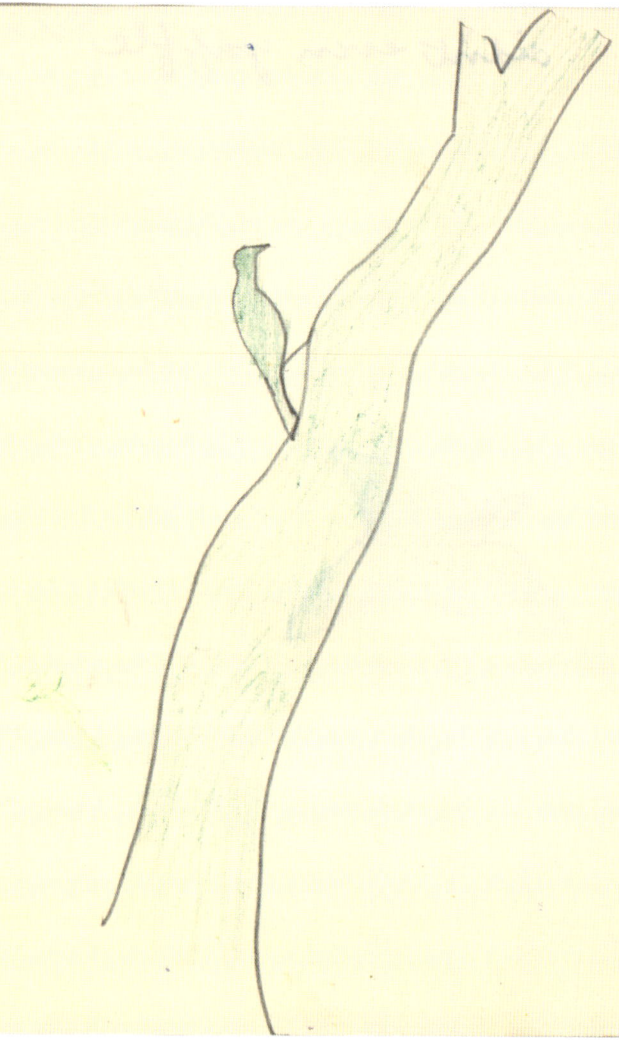

23rd

ords & Ladies' Lollipops

he ping of milk into a pail,
he first squirt, — then the
ing, ting, ring ing in the cool
dark.

a blood Red admiral

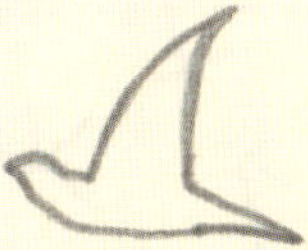

Flete, — beloved, very, very
dearey.

ne big, bored bull.

28th July

Tuesday to the hills
– The hikers' Hayfield
The rucksack-rounded hills

Bus to Buxton
for the china tea
that wasn't nice
& cakes that didn't come

rucksack wanderers
& the afternoon teaers
with cherried hats like cakes

The country green, green
always green
& blackveined by the walls

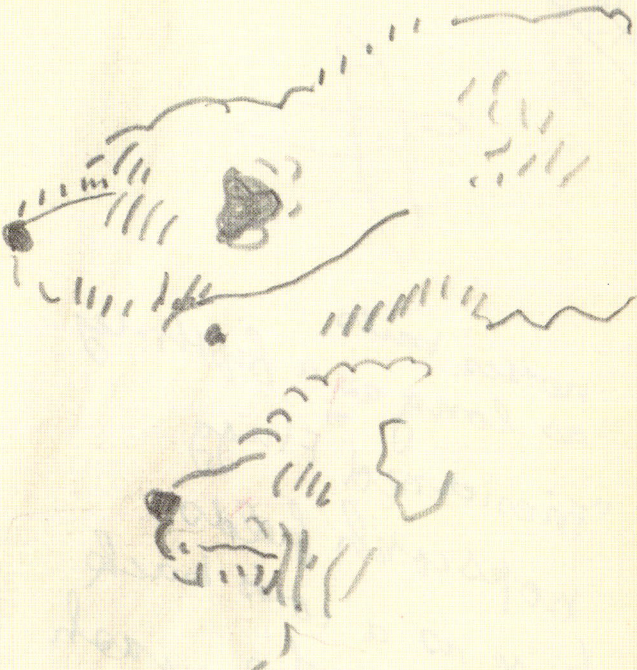

The wind is turning
the sycamore leaves.
The air – like washday

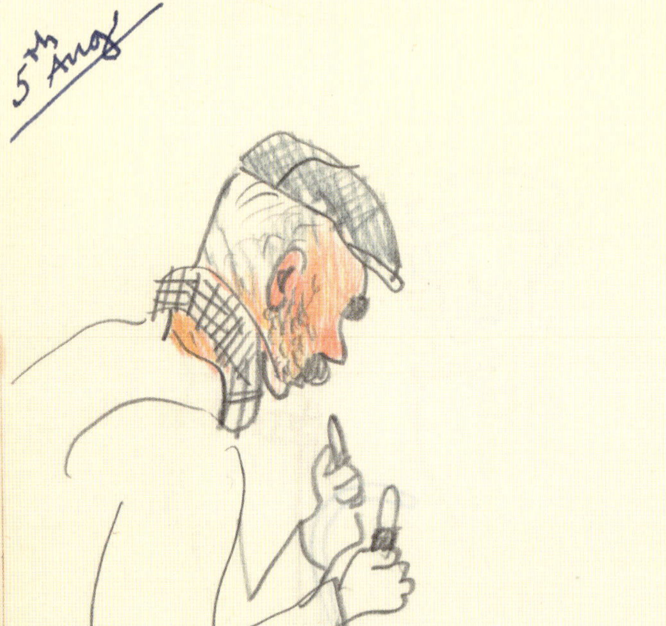
5th Aug
Longnor

6th

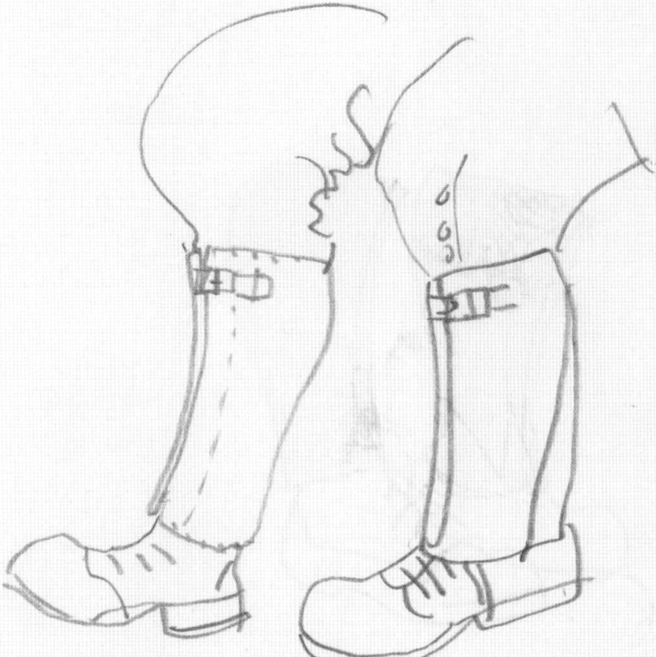

Blue Boar black boots
& brown laces

The Minster sounds
The secondhand books smell

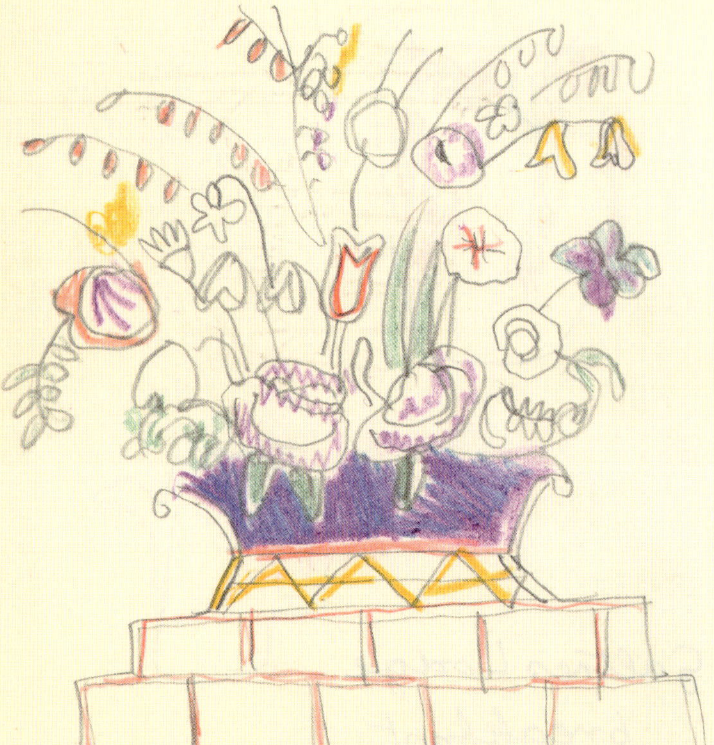

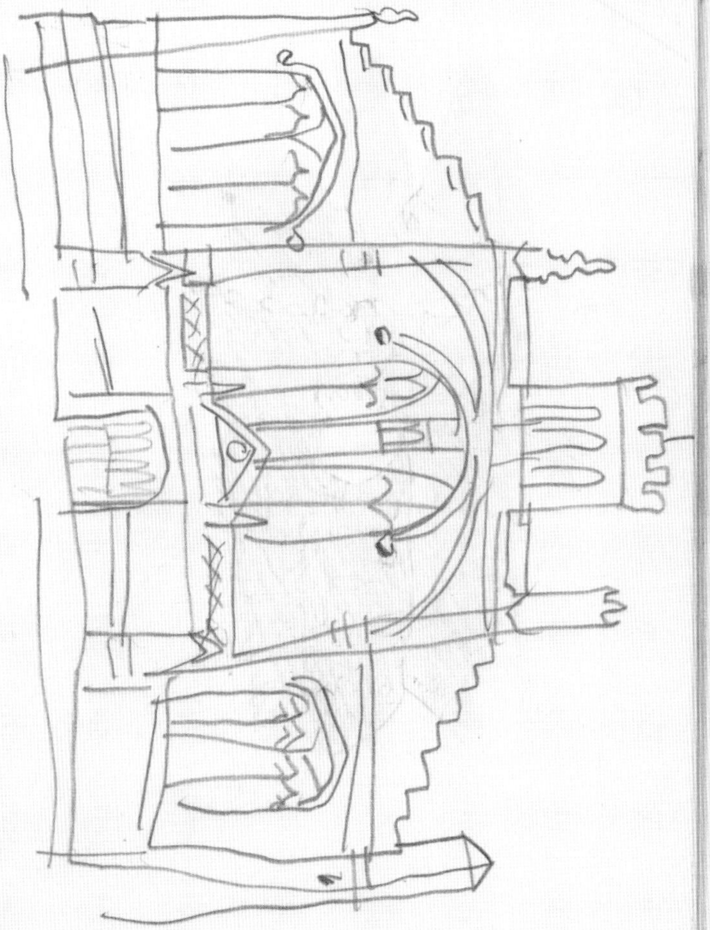

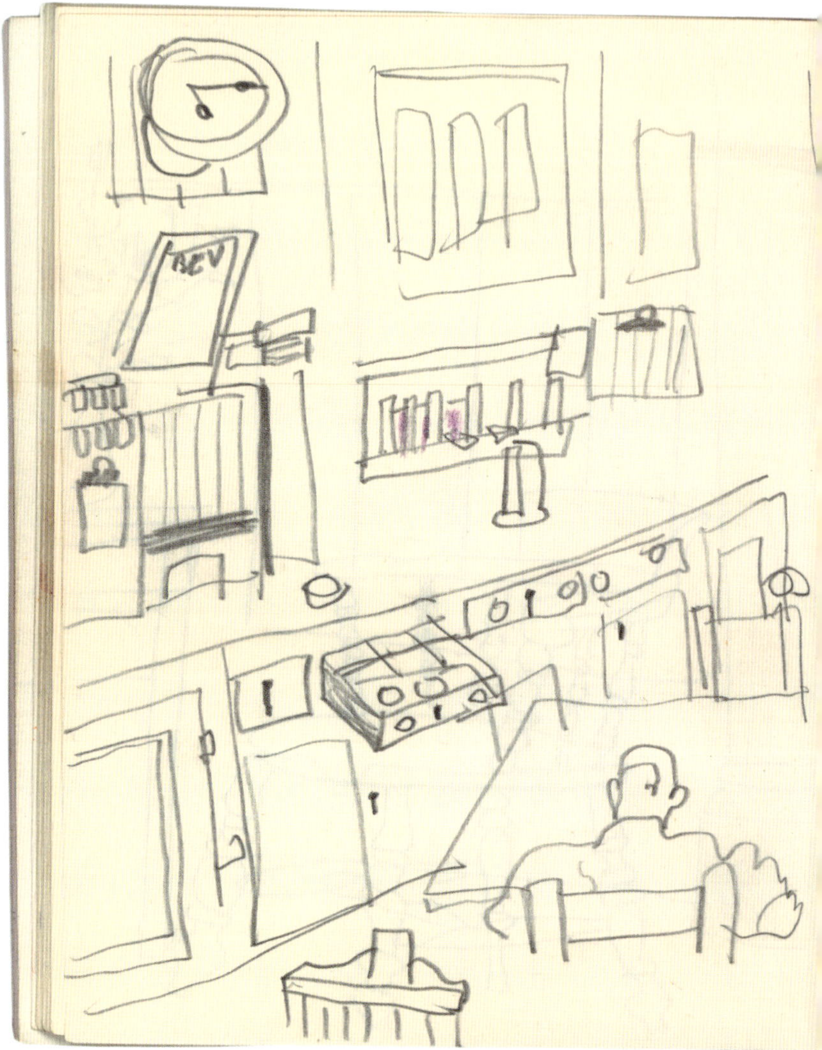
BEV

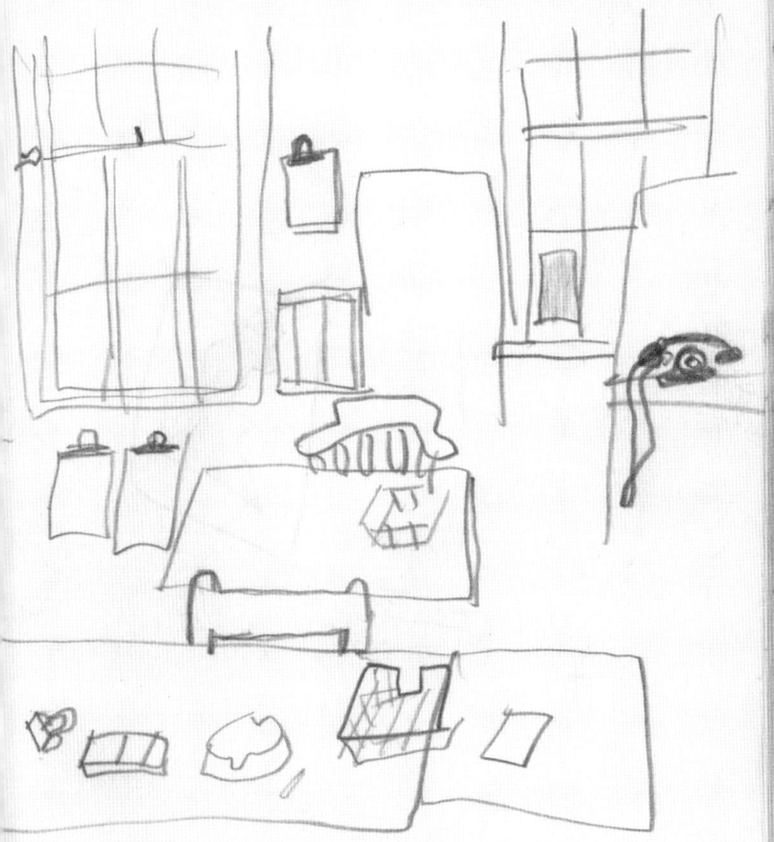

Train Departures
from Beverley.

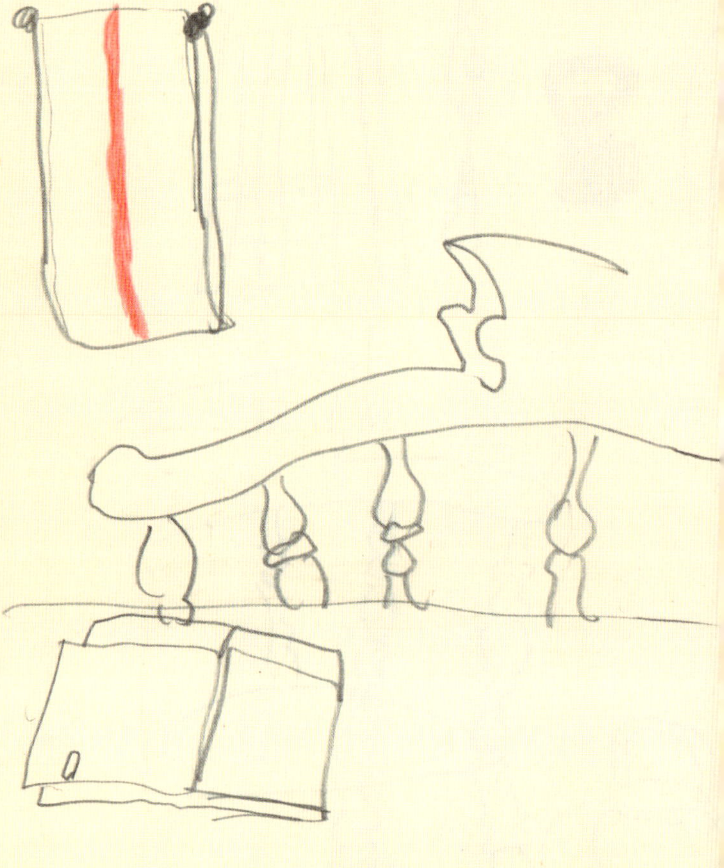

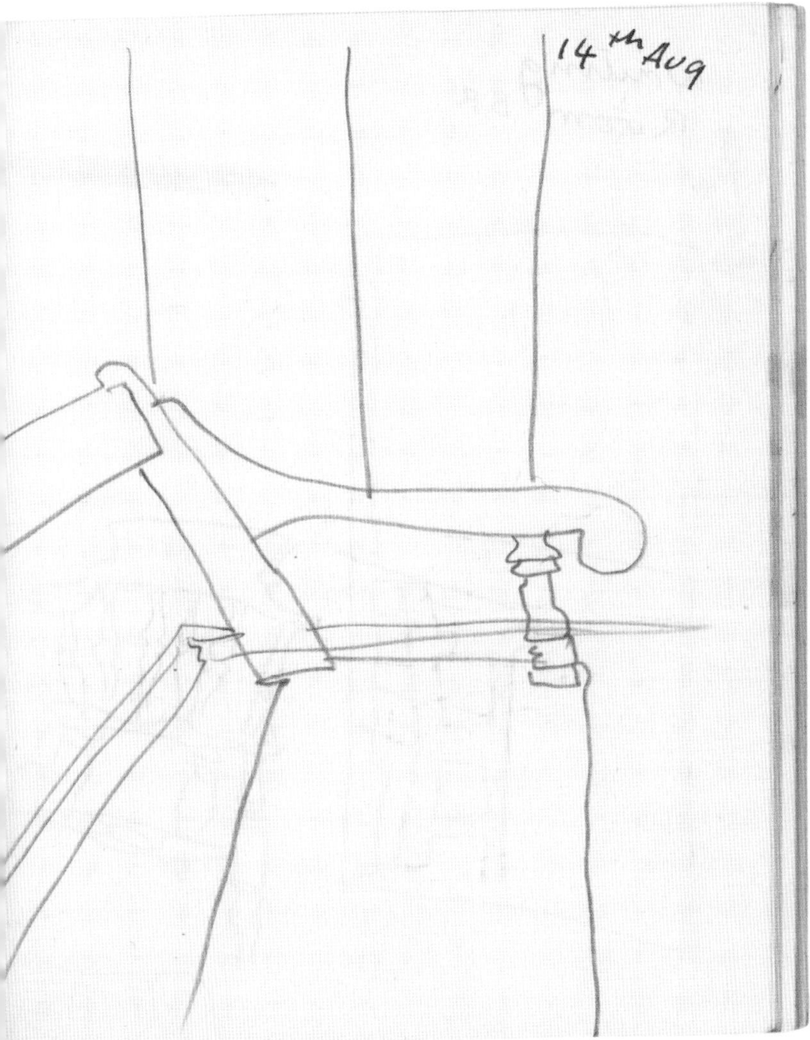
14th Aug

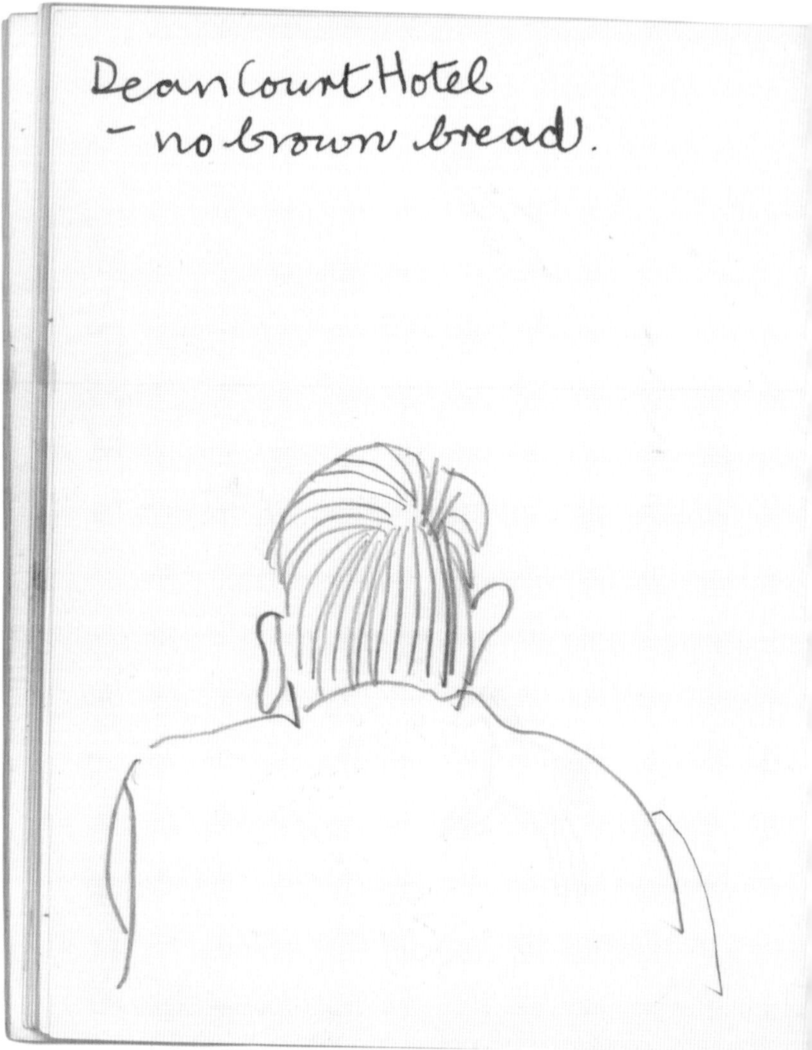
Dean Court Hotel
– no brown bread.

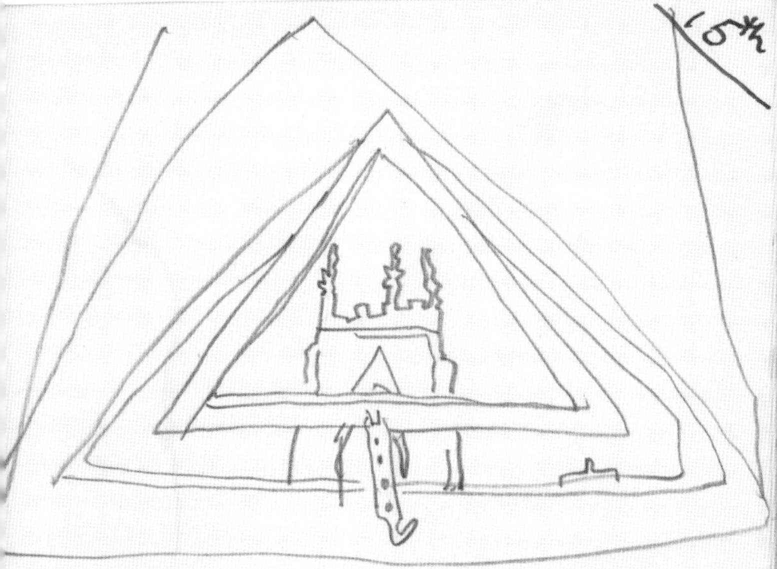

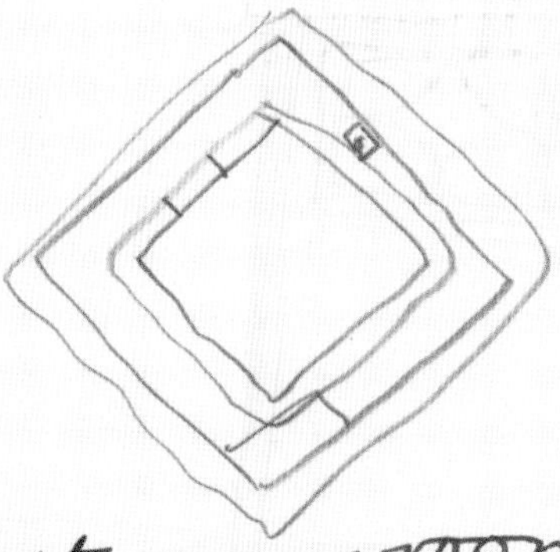

Dean Court – my room

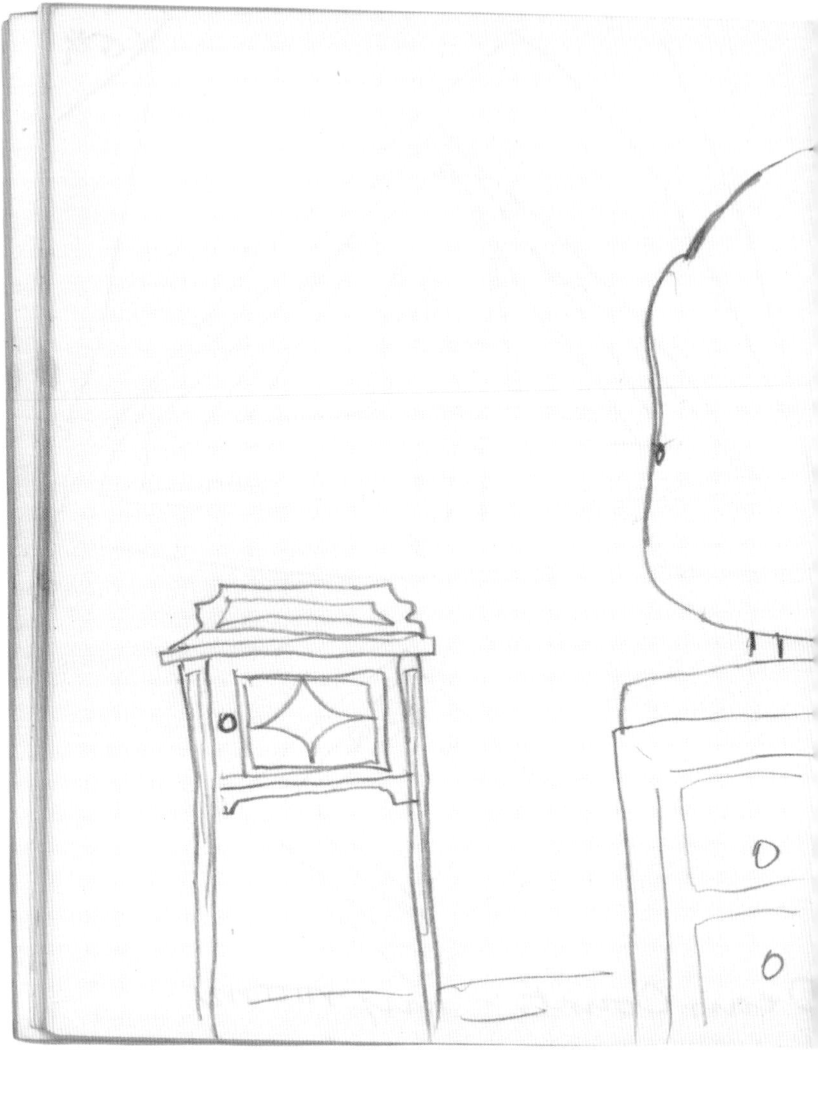

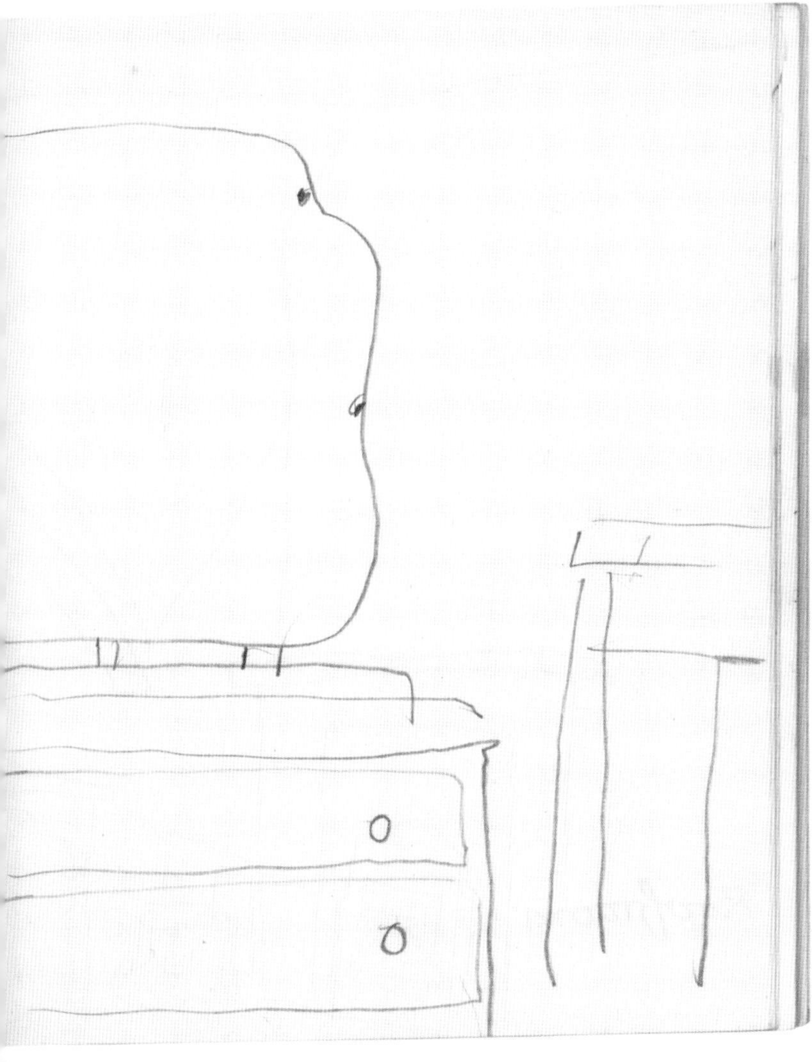

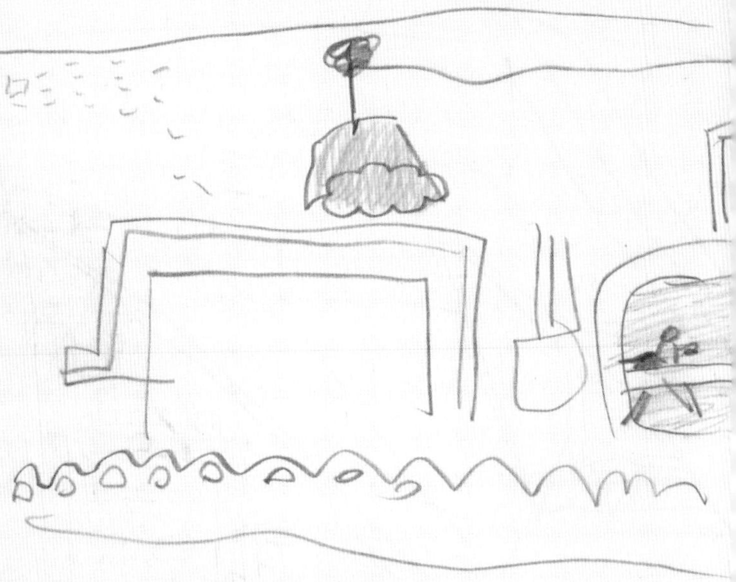

The Golden Slipper
Goodramgate
The 2.45
Three o'clock beer stakes
Saturday afternoon

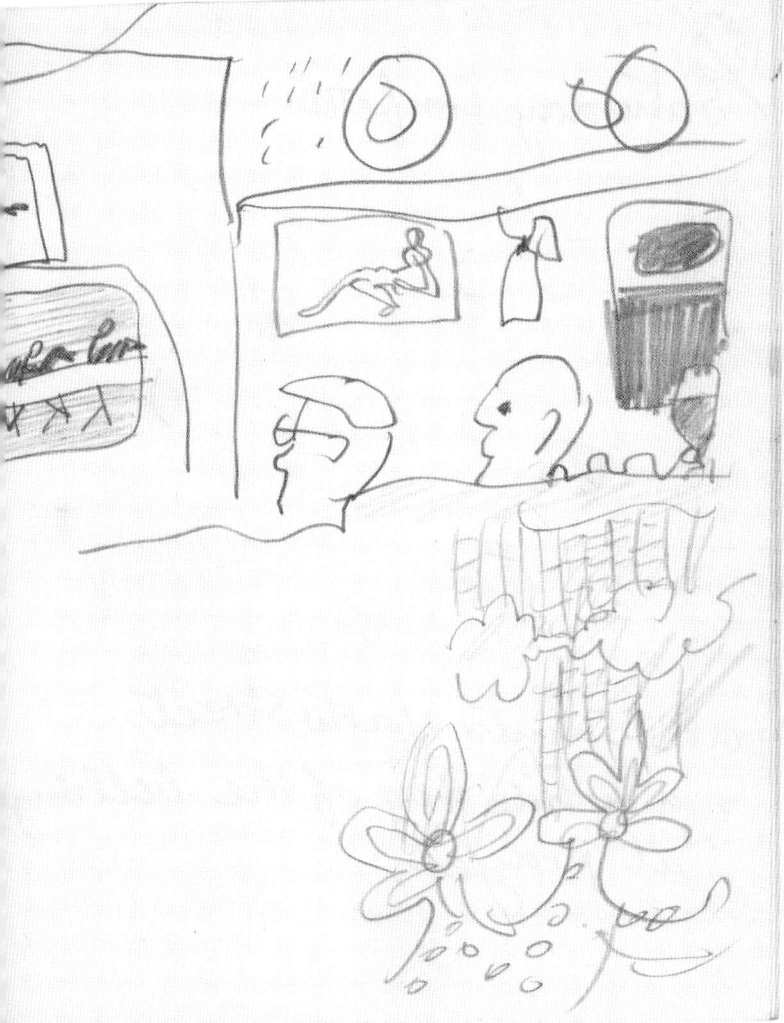

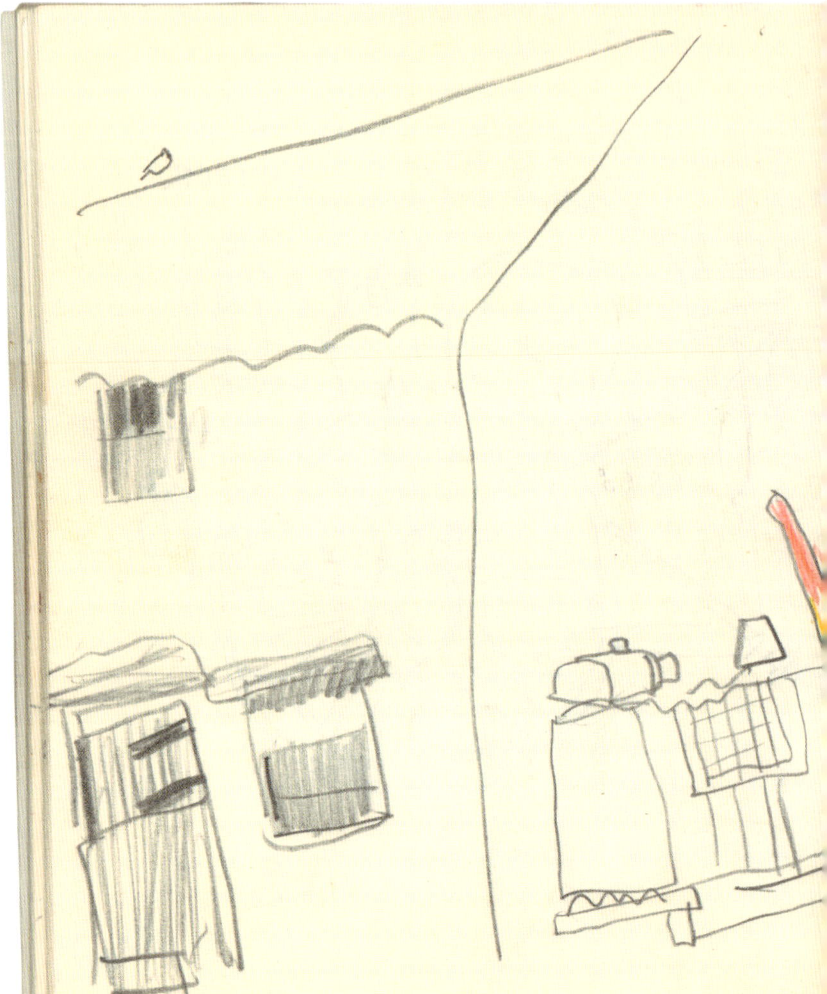

"Gat sumrat poison in there"

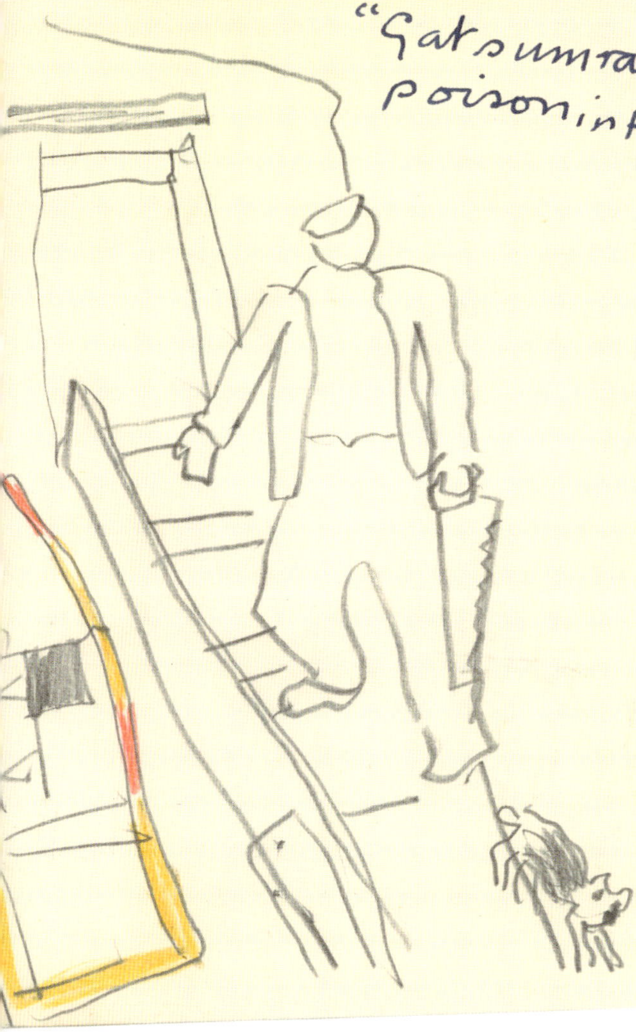

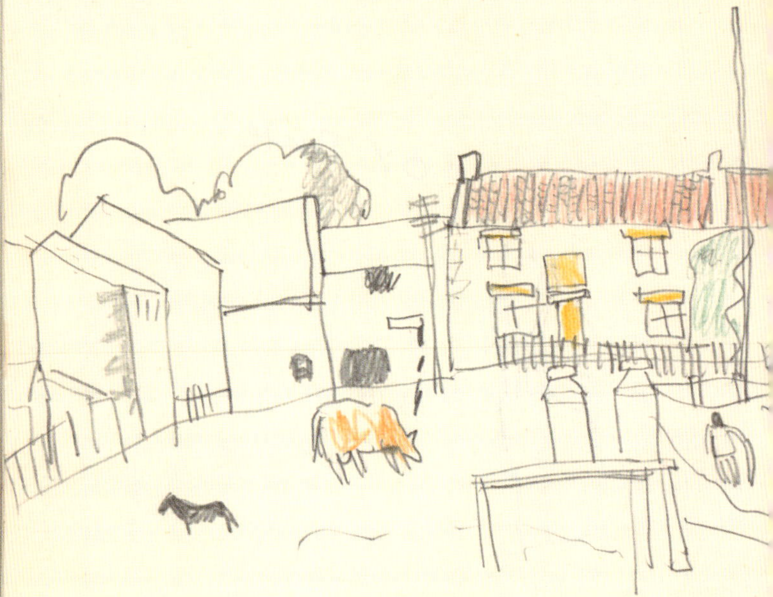

The village street is as
eventful as the village flagpole

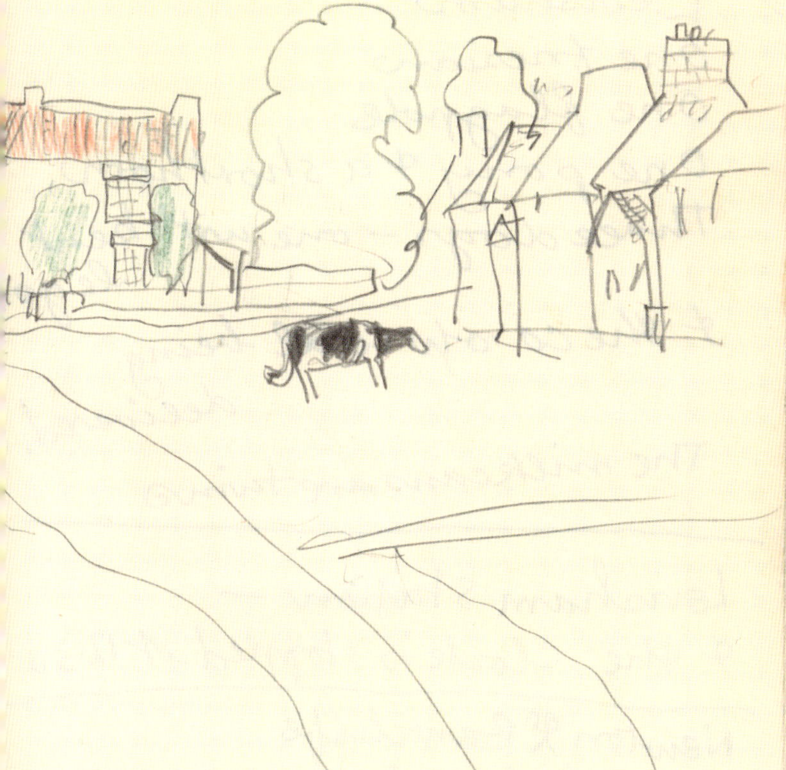

as straight

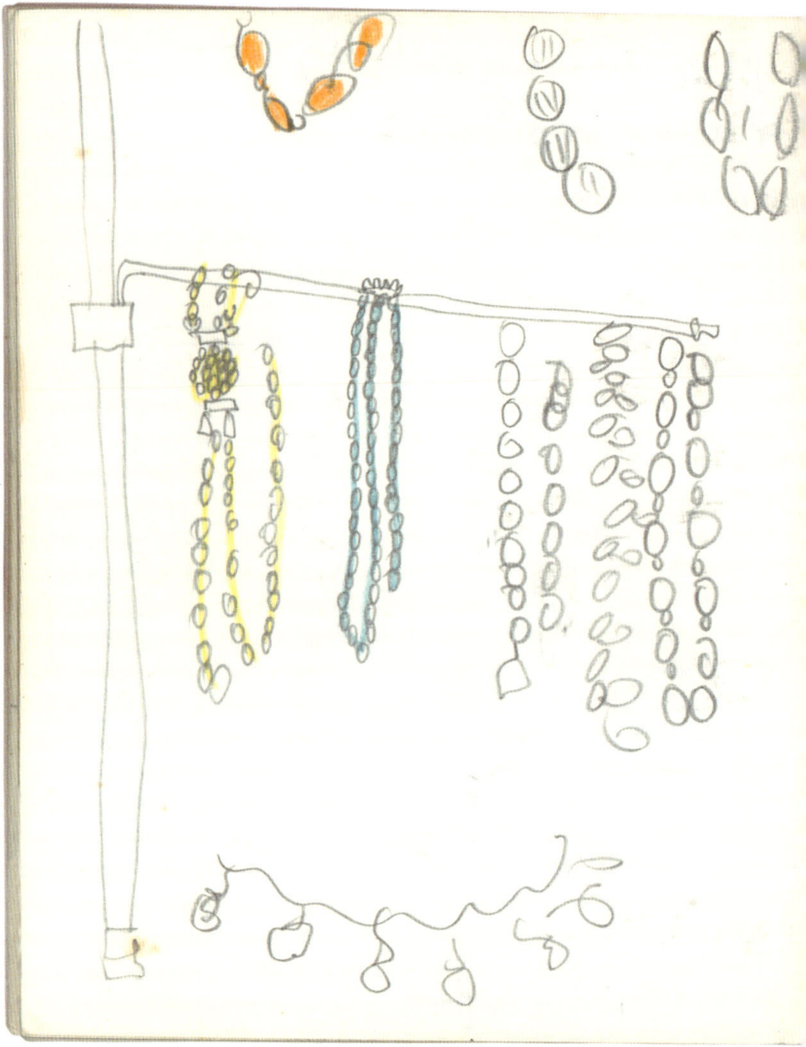

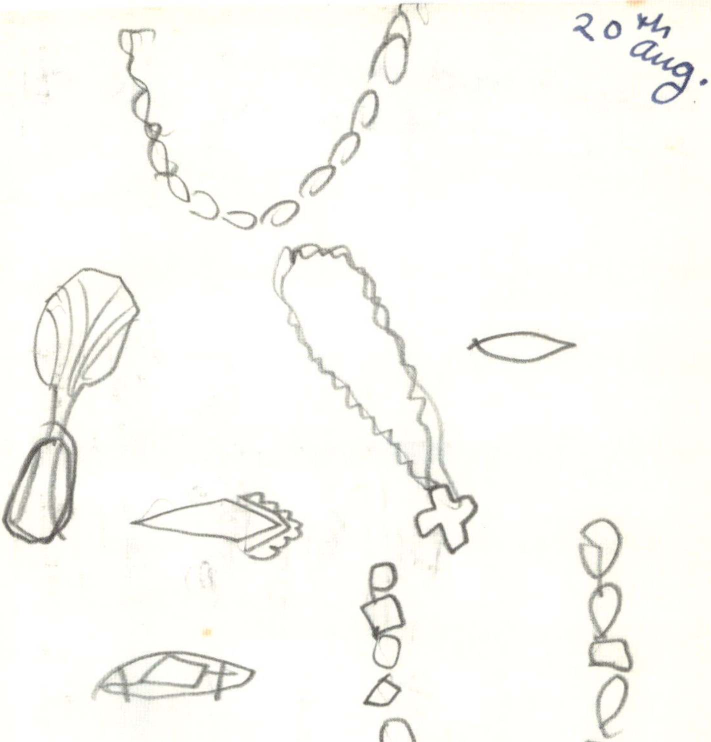
20th aug.
Real Whitby jet

22nd august

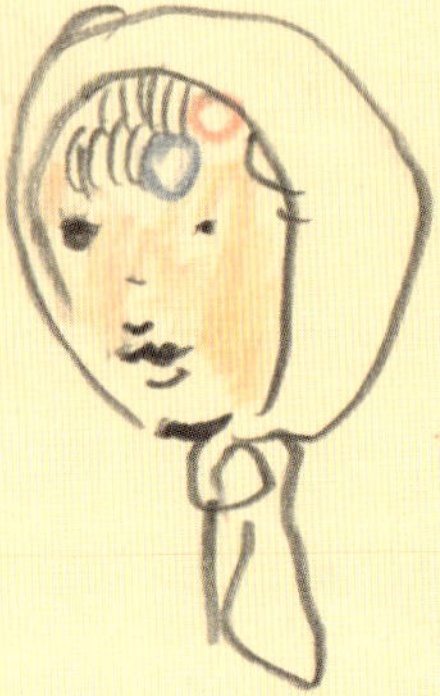

miss middleton
curling pins

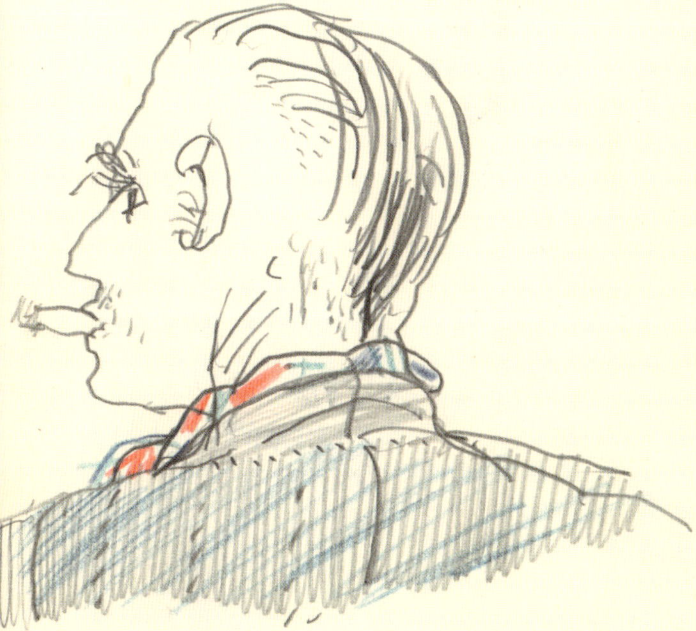

green racing special

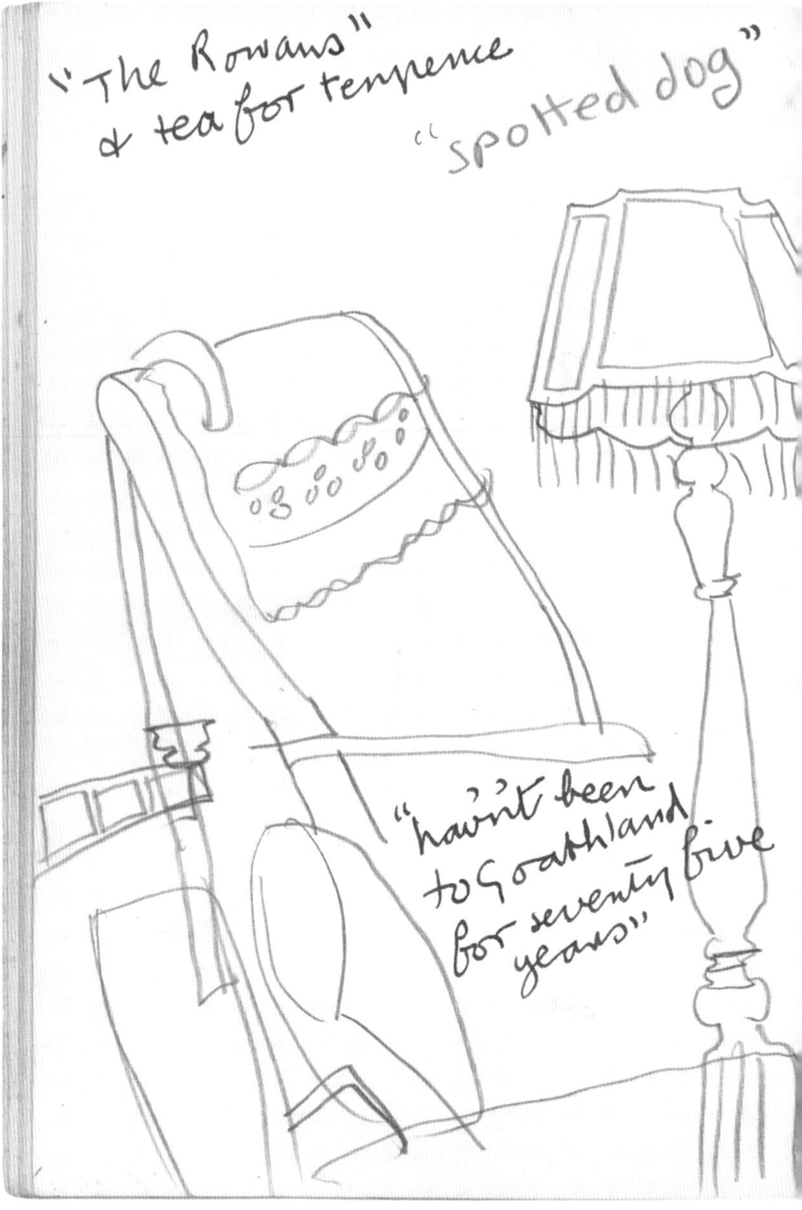
"The Rowans"
& tea for tenpence
"spotted dog"
"havin't been
to Goathland
for seventy five
years"

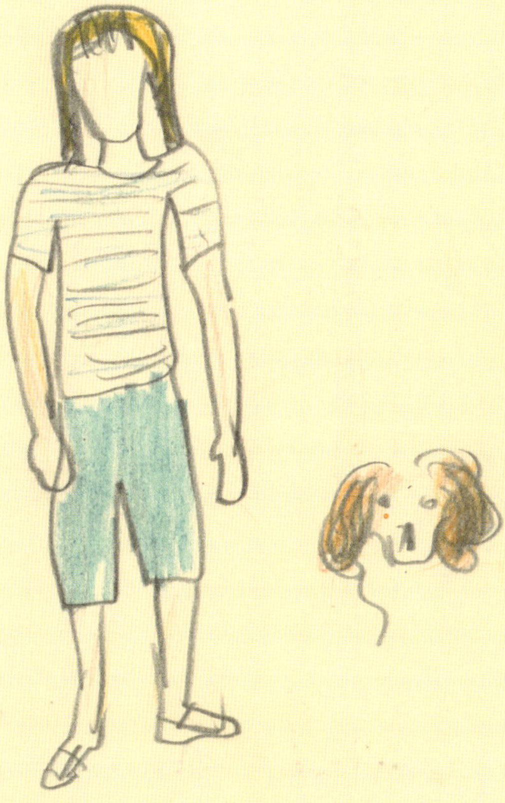

Saxon Cowherd
— Lewisham

24th august

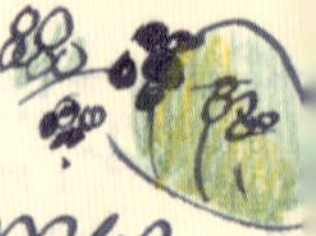

The first black, blackberries
& the smell of Monday's morning suds
harvests of brown bread
in the baker's window.
Pickering on
Monday market Day

muffin munchers on the train
& soft drinkers of coloured wat
& bent straws trapped in
empty bottles
comic cutters, ham rollers
& hand knitters & the
nibblers of potatoes crisps

To Mellor via Sheffield
& Stony Middleton.
~~Buxton~~ & Cheetham Hill
Millers Dale

25th

I smell the august plums
stewing

– Back to the country of the
magpies, & the ~~land~~ place
of childhood's blackberry-
picking; apple pie on
Saturdays & Farmer Granny's
famous cream.
– the Tounscliffe strong tea
& the cloth on the table
cornerways
boiled eggs hard

8th sept

Rotting rhododendron leaf mosa

In the gateway .....
the dry earth with bits of sticks of stra
& a wind from the sea.

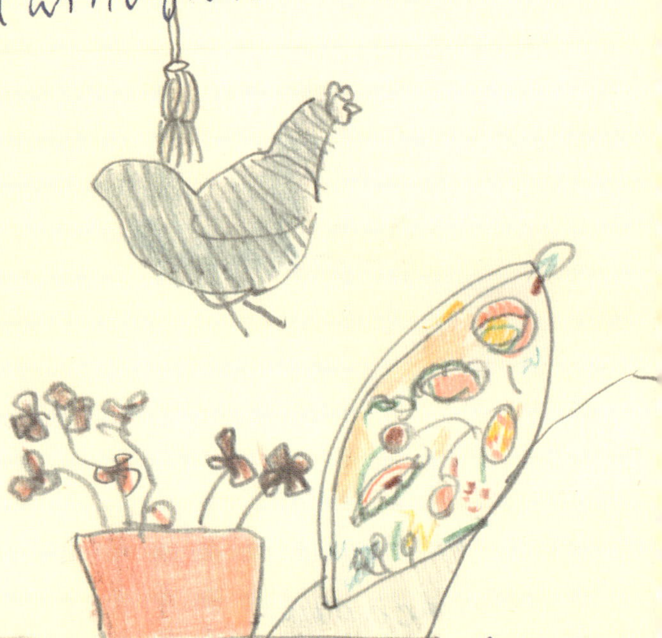

Scholars returning on their bus
from the new term in new blazers
The time of autumn fruits in jar
conkers, hips & guelder roses red

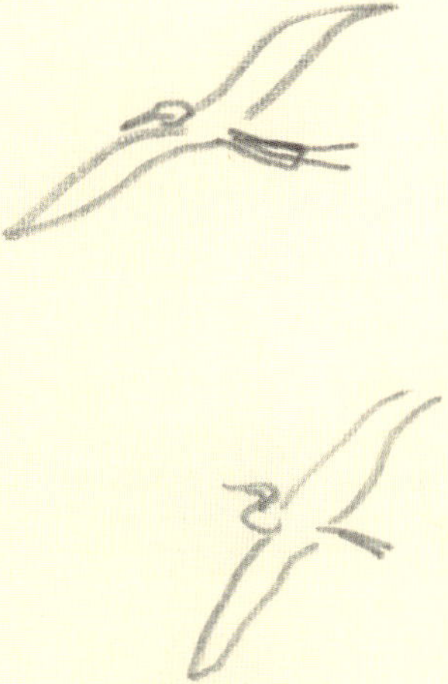

Again Fleté

Past the Privaté Notices.

walked to Holbeton

& bought a box of matches 2½d

jars on the window cills

20th

Trinity XVII

Turkeys on my roof

Archipelagos of white clouds in the clearest blue

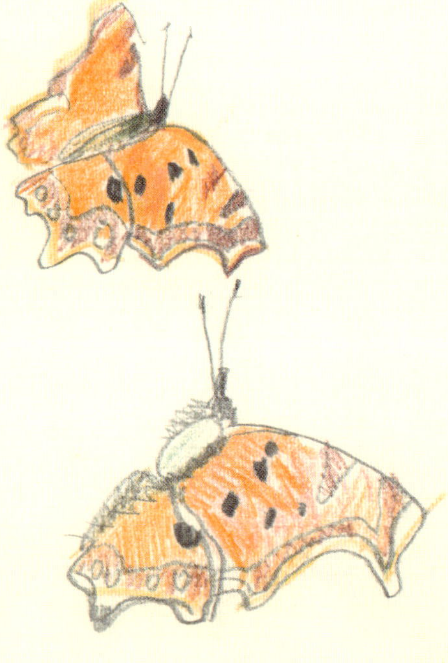

20th

berry-ripe-time
nuthedgetime

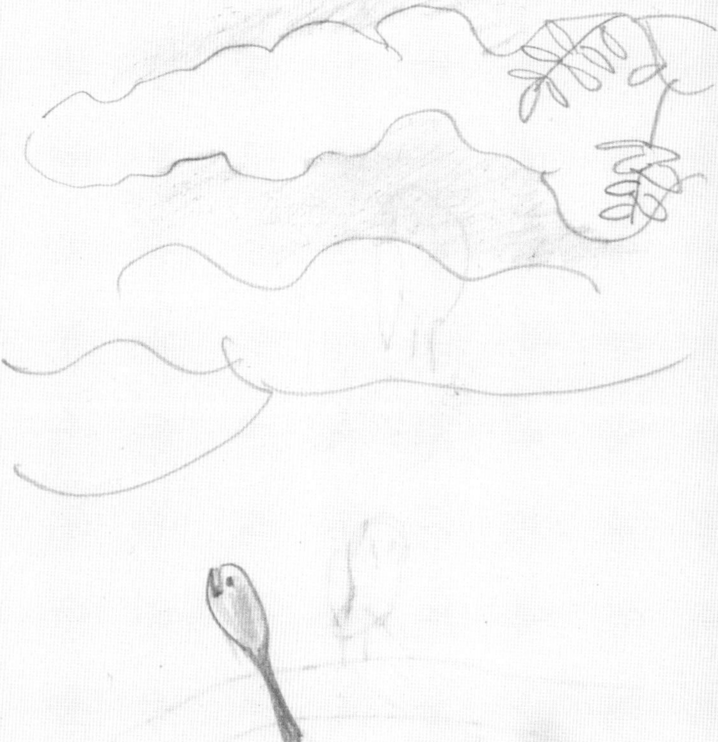

Tits, Tits, Tits, Tits,
—Longtailed

Mrs House waves her brush
at the turkey on my roof

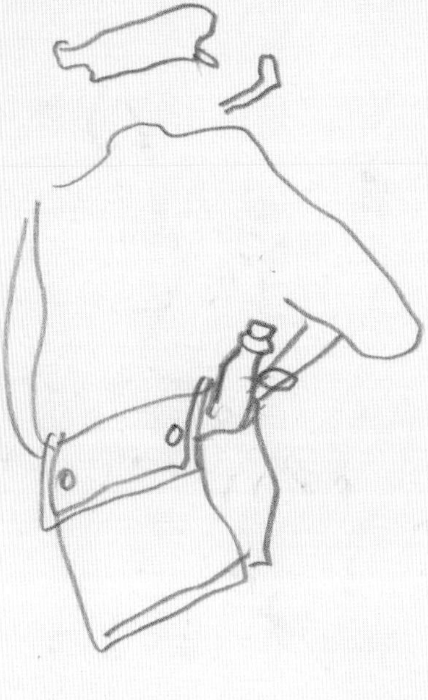

21st sept

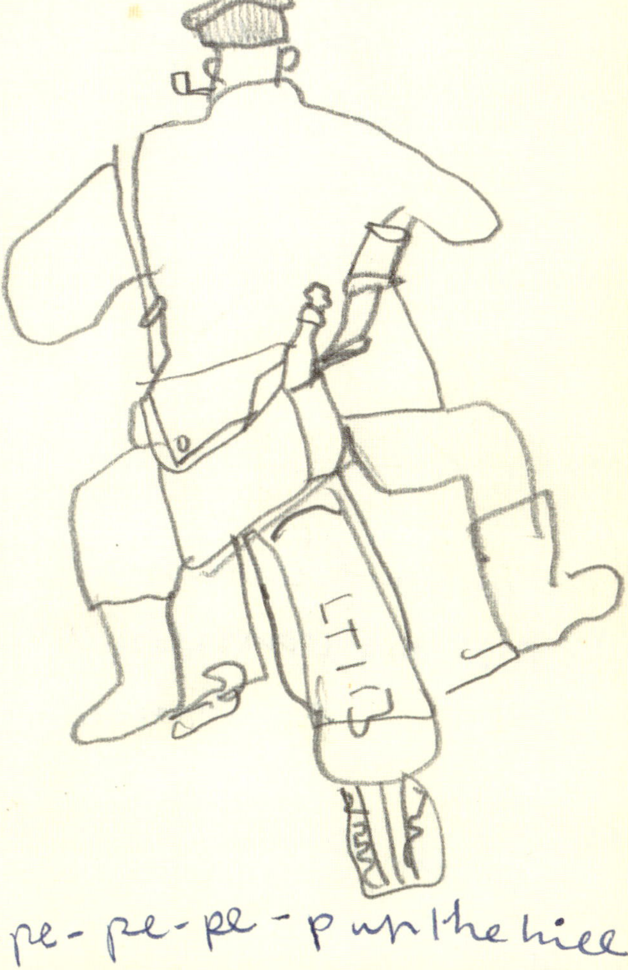

pe-pe-pe-pe-p up the hill

Still September's summer

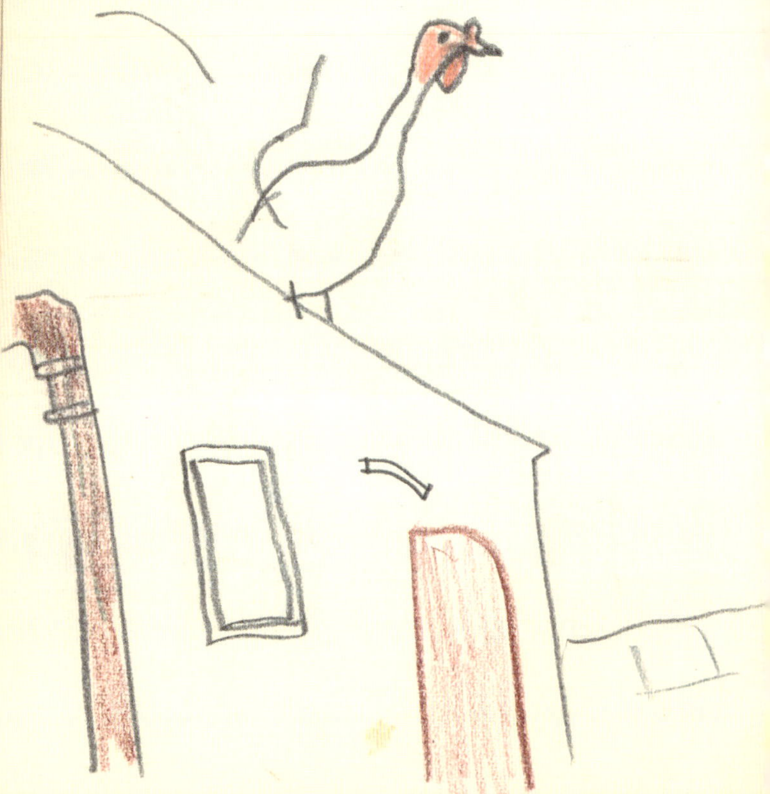

26th Sept

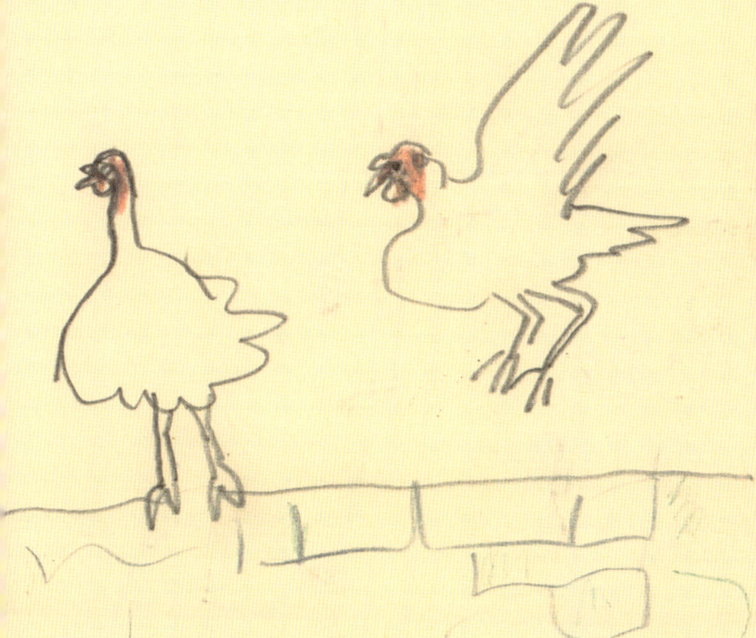

Saturday
Visitors

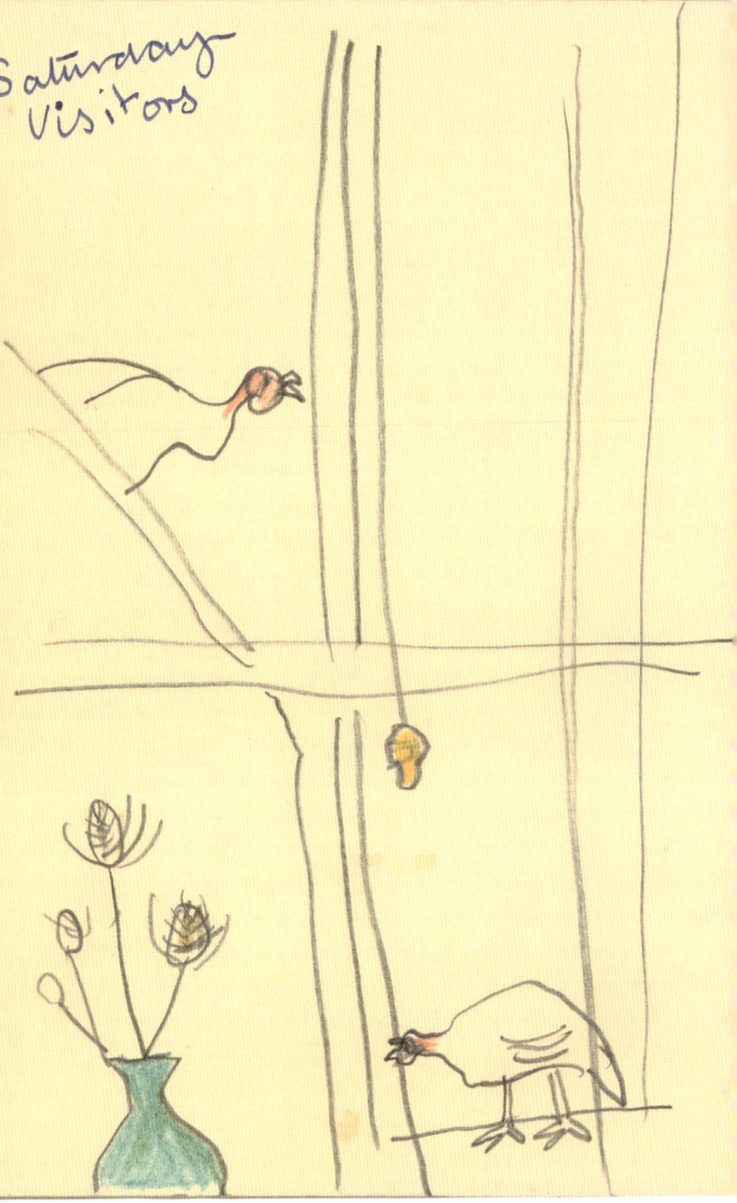

27th

Trinity XVIII

"The Harvest"

Jars of jam,
& jam jars harvest-full
of Michaelmas flowers
& one that crashes in the Sermon!

The rosy apples' specially red.

Heat of the Summer
& stillness of September

Eggs on the Lady Chapel altar
&
the marrows on the Strashleigh
Tomb.

& an offering of oranges –
& tomatoes in their home-grown
glory

18th Nov.

Week of wetness,
& a new beauty —
that of brown autumn & winte
gnats, bats,
a smell of cigarette
at dusk.

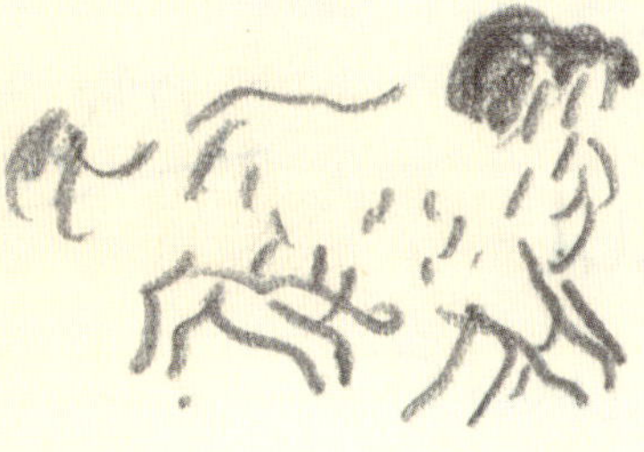

The dock leaf, the dandelion,
& the cow in the field

19th

The leaves are gone
the landscape winter-looking

29th NOV

Advent 1

Suddenly cold
— & concious of the church heat,
collars up & Wind East

Cup of tea at Penquit

Advent II

6th Dec.

Wind & the window
rattling, damp & the
drizzle coming down.

Three years of Sundays
at Ermington

10th

a porch in the sun -
the Keeper's Lodge
& 'sporting' hens

1965

11 Jan.

not a blackbird
– but a pram's squeaking
song in the road.

2nd February

The daylight favourably
longer.

~~7th~~

Epiphany V first primroses
"Nice & Dry" Preston Lane

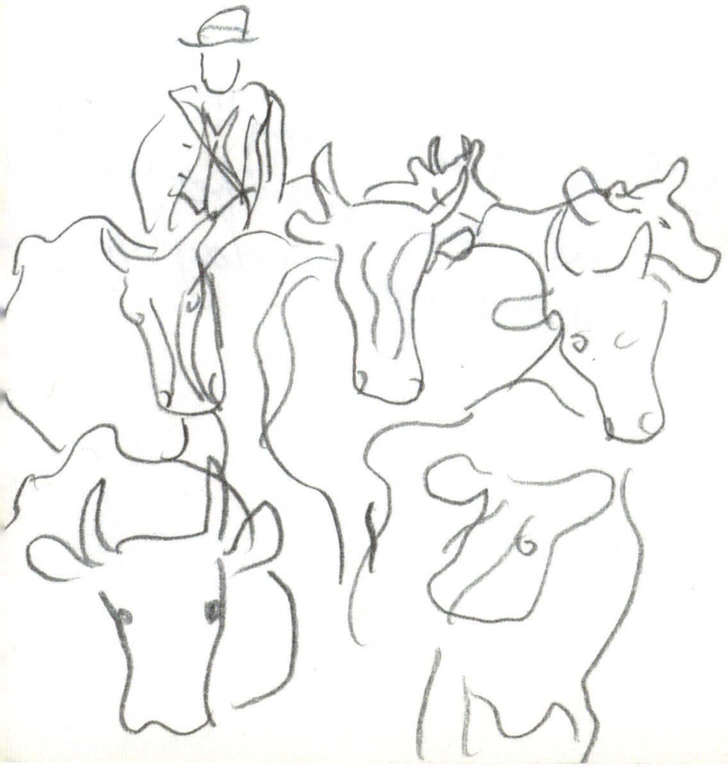

14th Feb.

Septuagesima
The Bishop Celebrates
a sniff of spring air
& two dark violets
all things bright & beautiful

15th Feb.

over the wall —
Mr Tall giving the hens
all but his knife & fork;
Monday's sunday leftovers.

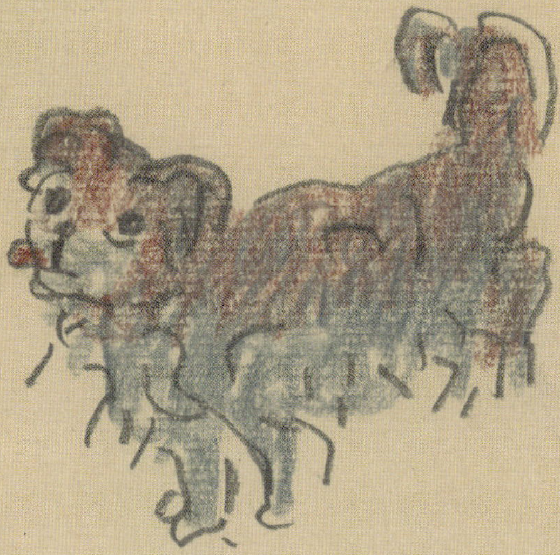

28th Feb.

Quinquagesima,
& the last day of a dry month – rather dampish.
Celebration at 8.00am by the Bishop – & a dinner of brawn.

The would-be-blue hyacinth is opening – & its a pink one.

March 1 & all sorts of weather.

Larks & lambs – both singing on the way to a Modbury haircut.

March 1st

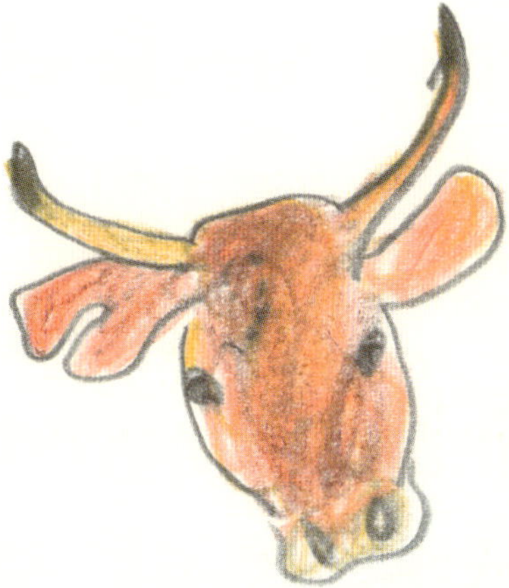

3rd March

ash Wednesday –
wildest ash Wednesday,
wind & rain & severe all day

7 March

W. on Sunday
for the Misses Johns
Quadragesima left, right

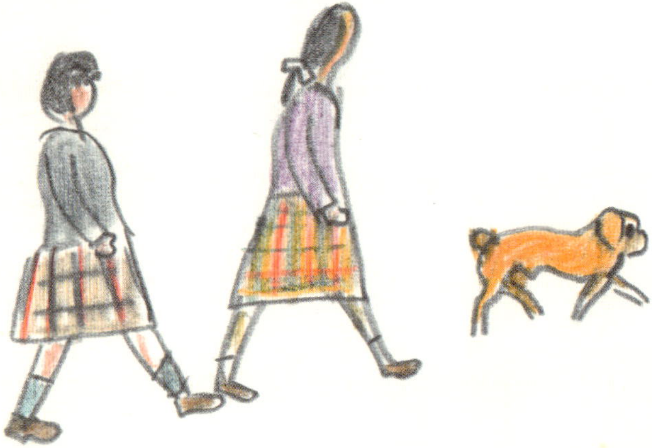

The Sun! & windows open. 8th March

Rooks sound as though they are house hunting

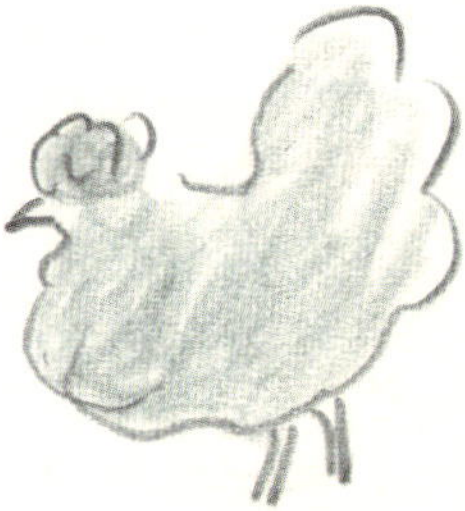

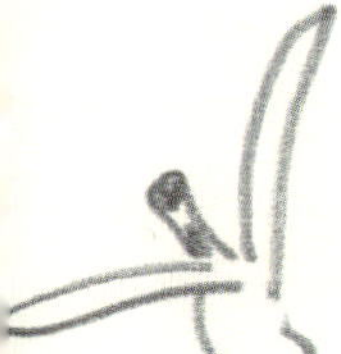

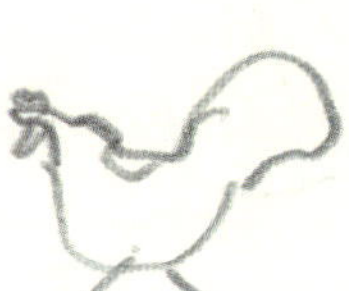

24th March blowing drier.

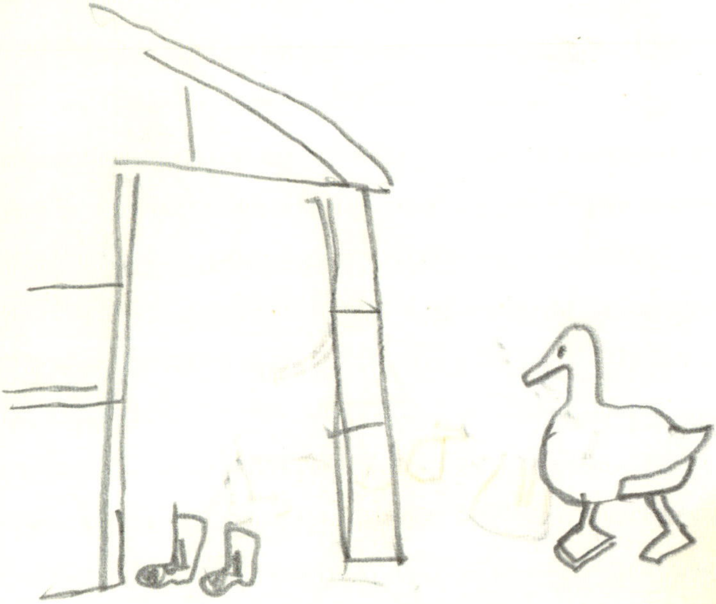

Lady Day

25th March

Green jelly for breakfast
West wind & the celandines shut
"monk's lunch"
& caught by the rain

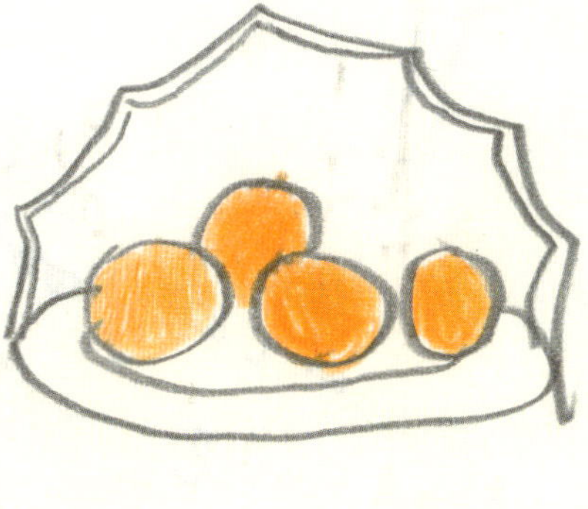

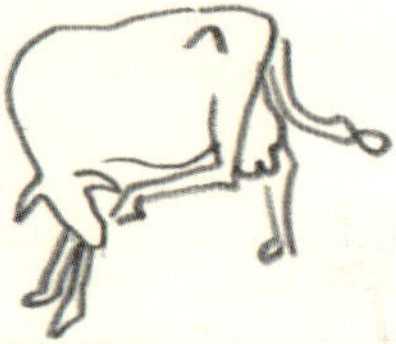

Kissing the sun - the celandines

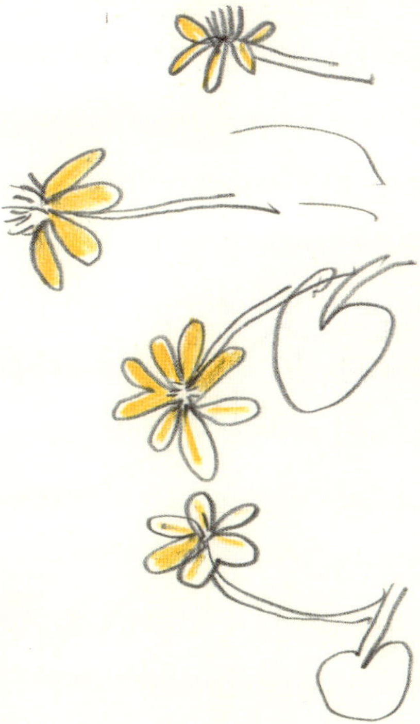

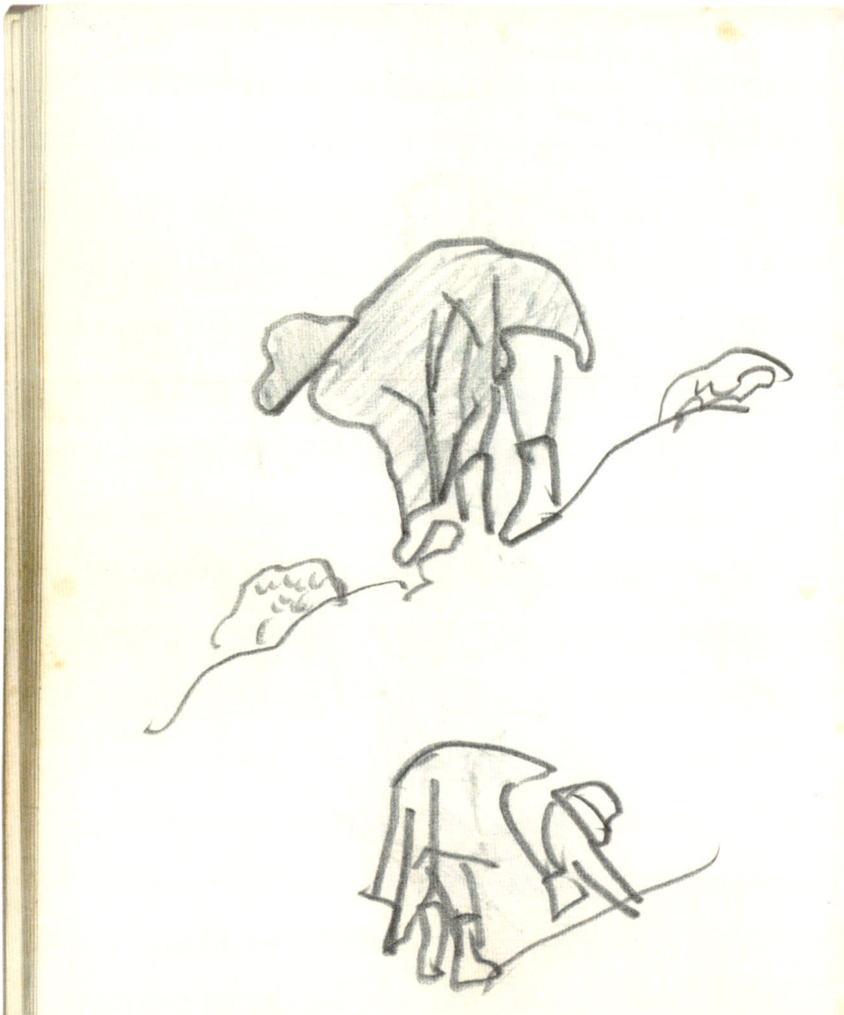

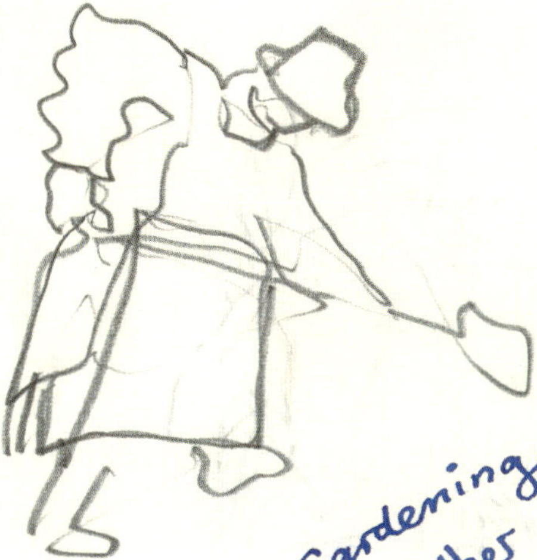

Gardening
weather it is

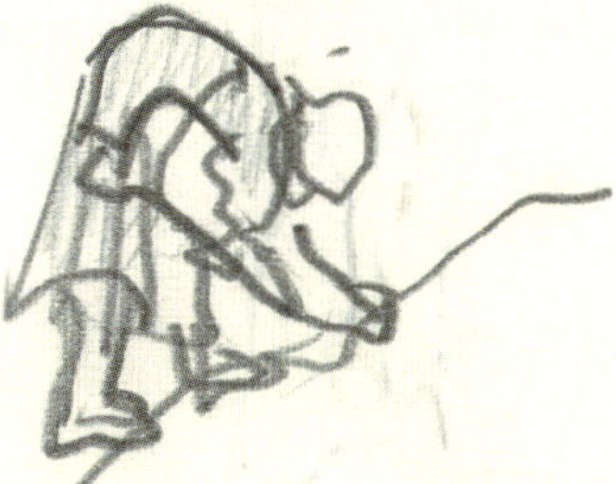

12th april

Rectory Cottager

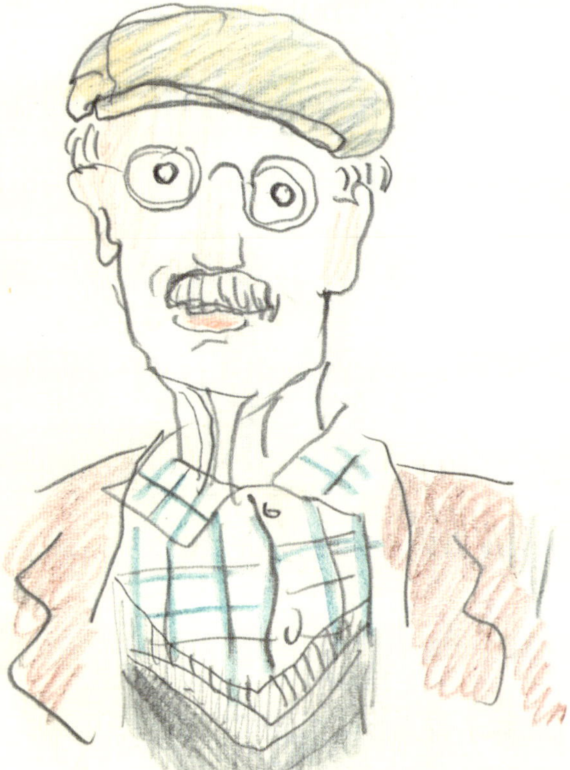

started in his garden

gardening beginning

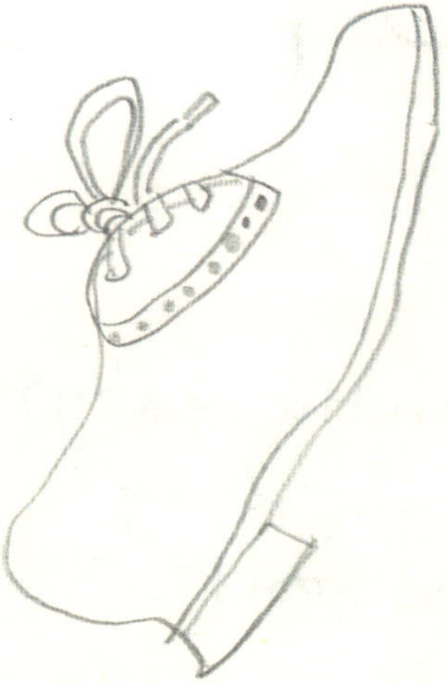

to mellor 13th April

12th May

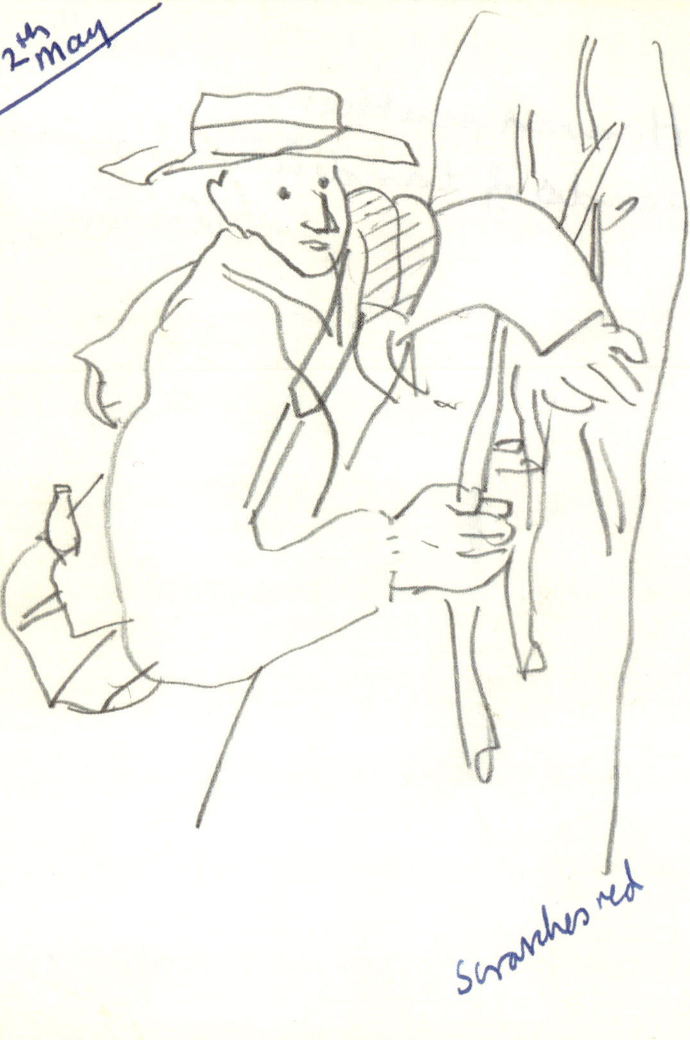

Scratches red

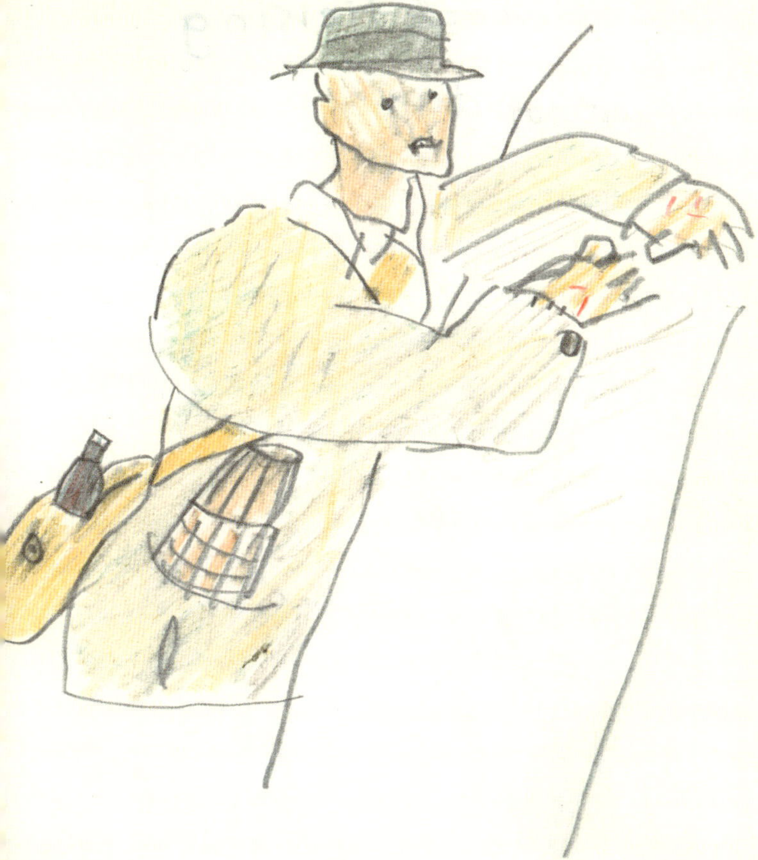

13th may

Time is the church clock ticking

lollipop days

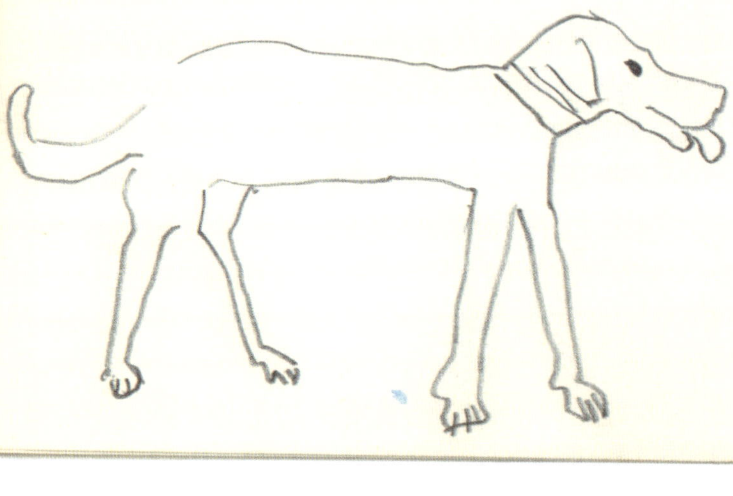

picnics-with-icecream-weather

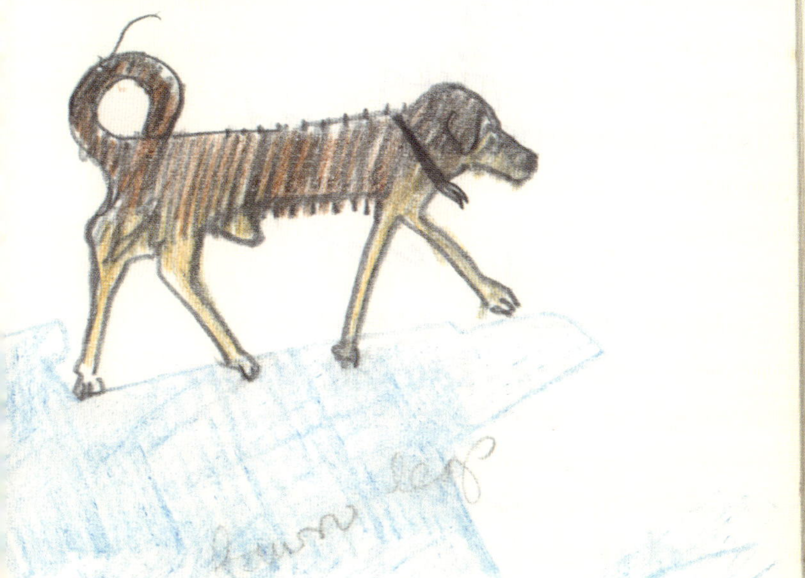

Pythagoras shadows
in the square —
all lessons in geometry

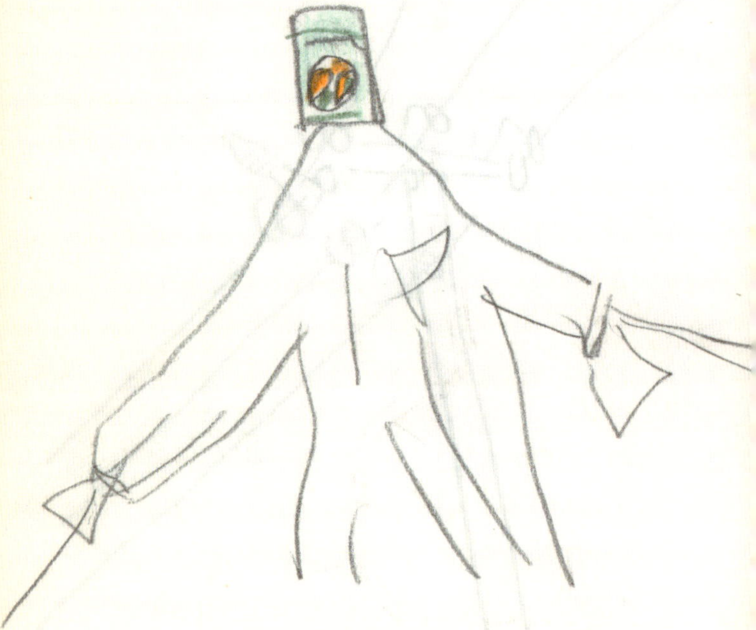

Carrot tin
Crow scare

I can walk to the island
in the river & be Robinson Crusoe

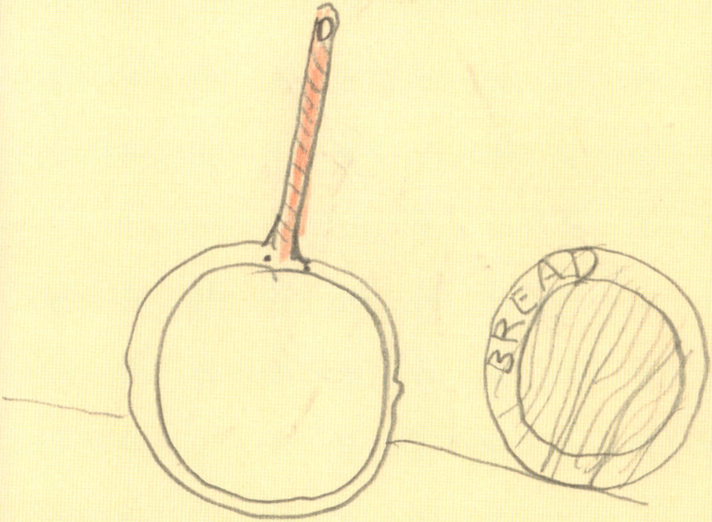

Friday
– drying the frying pan

After the sun-jungle smell
of the damp woods at Salkagrar.

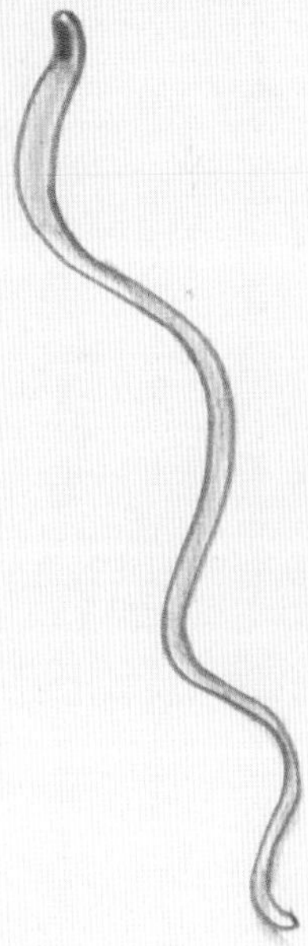

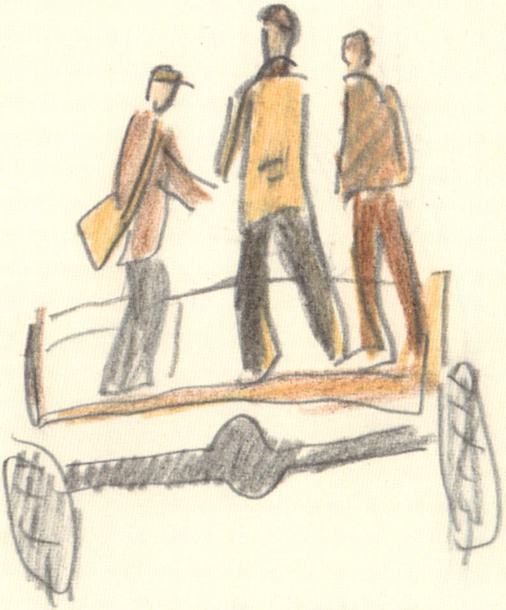

–lunch over

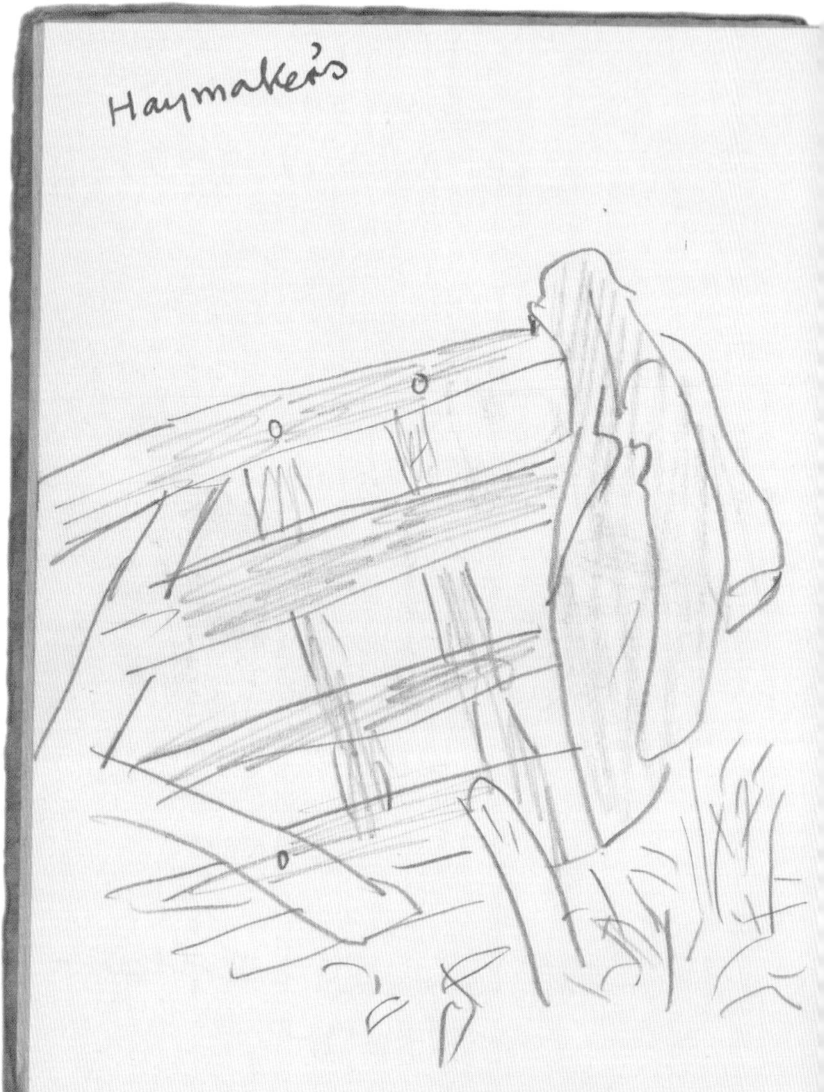
Haymaker's

11 June

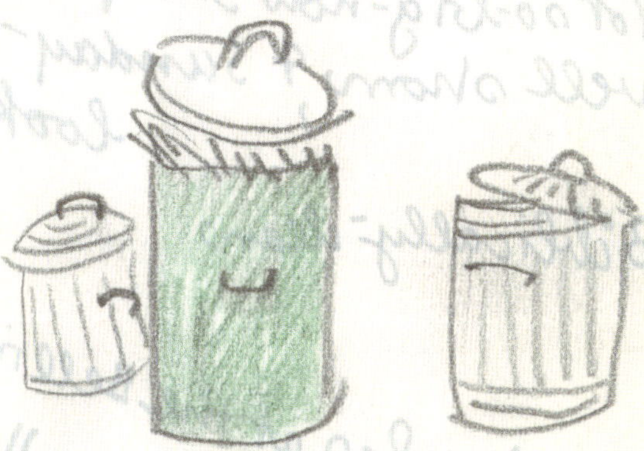

little brown mousehawk

balers thumping
& the yellowhammer's
song of "cheeeese"
afternoon "cheeeeese"

a real hay day

Great mullein's tower
of summer

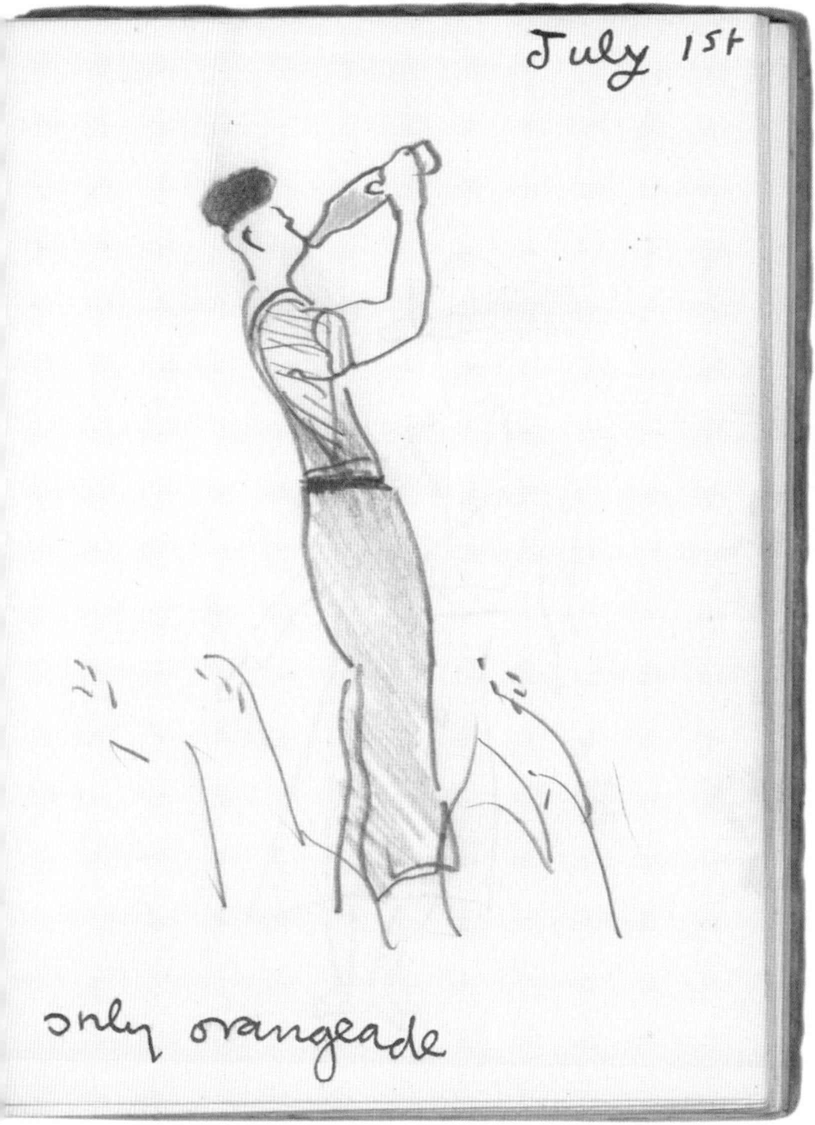
July 1st
only orangeade

12th July

Three day's rain;
The River is brown

13th

again, — rain
very much so.
Someone mowing the
River Field in the downpour
— swimming the
meadow.
Dark — ~~[illegible]~~ hear the River?

14 July

"9.18 on the other side"
Bridgewater – a cup of tea;
weak tea with the fields
wet from three days

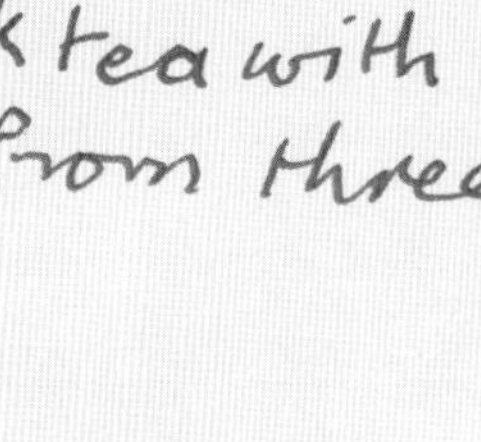

Shobdon 4.10pm

24th July

Methodist Fete at Milton

(17th Bible at Staunton on Arrow

Washing-up-ache

— an hour of it.

25th Trinity ~~VI~~ St James

Kingsland 8.00am

Pembridge 11.00 am

Bromyard 3.30 pm

Cream & Strawberries

No cheese, & ale

26th July

Midland Red 8.25 am

& Leominster Railway wait;

Antony & Cleopatra on the platform

And Stockport........

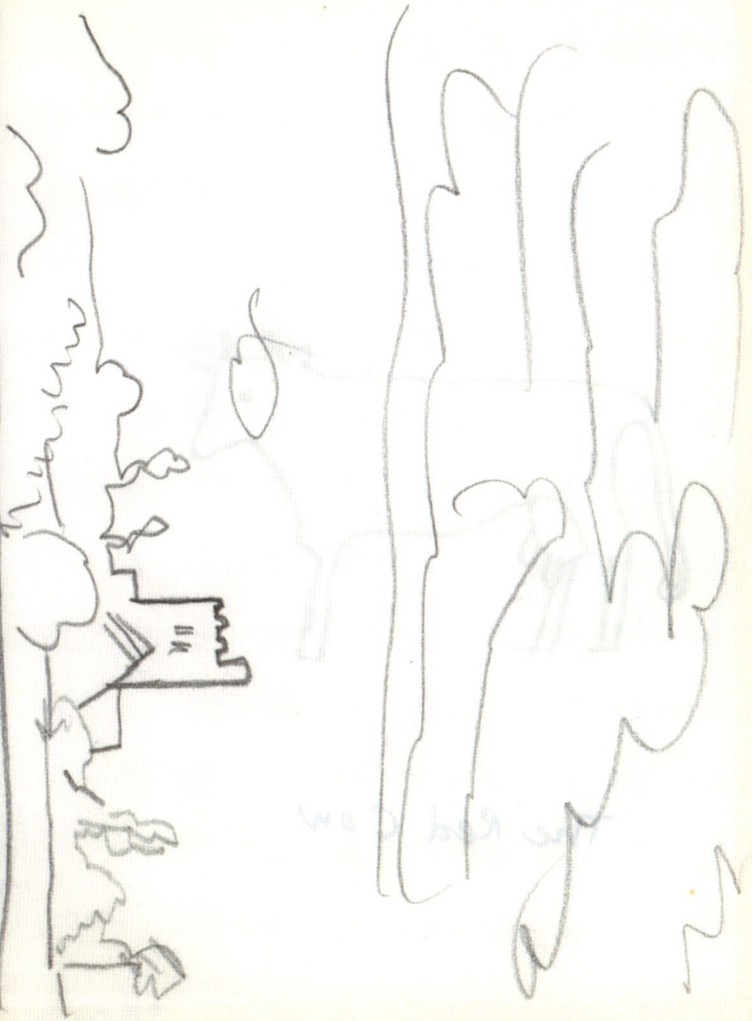

Walpole S. Andrews
- offered a push bike

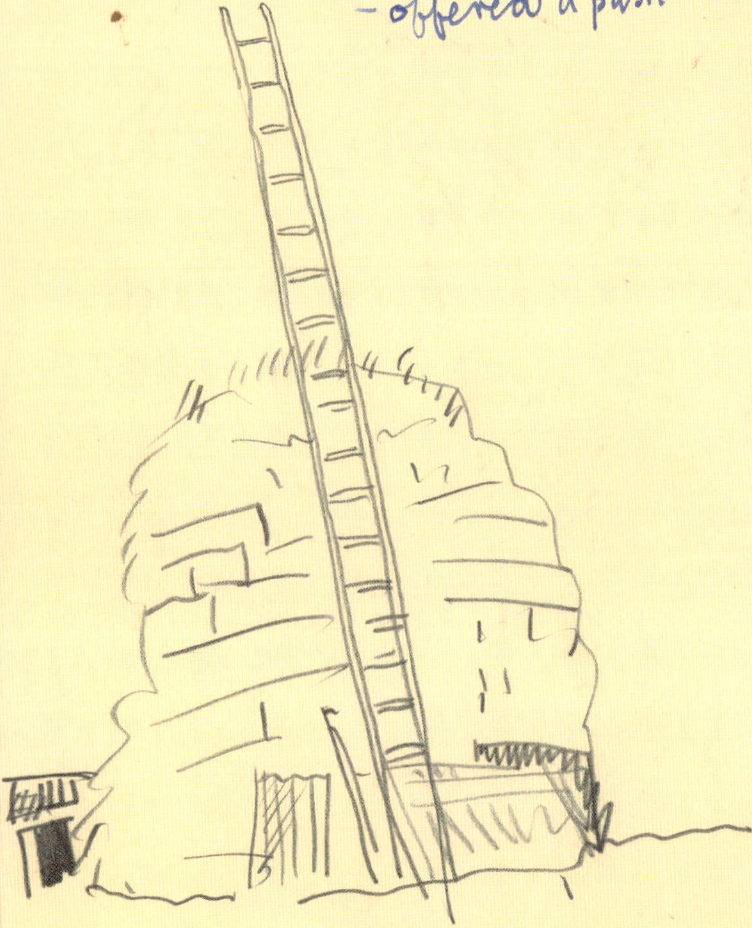

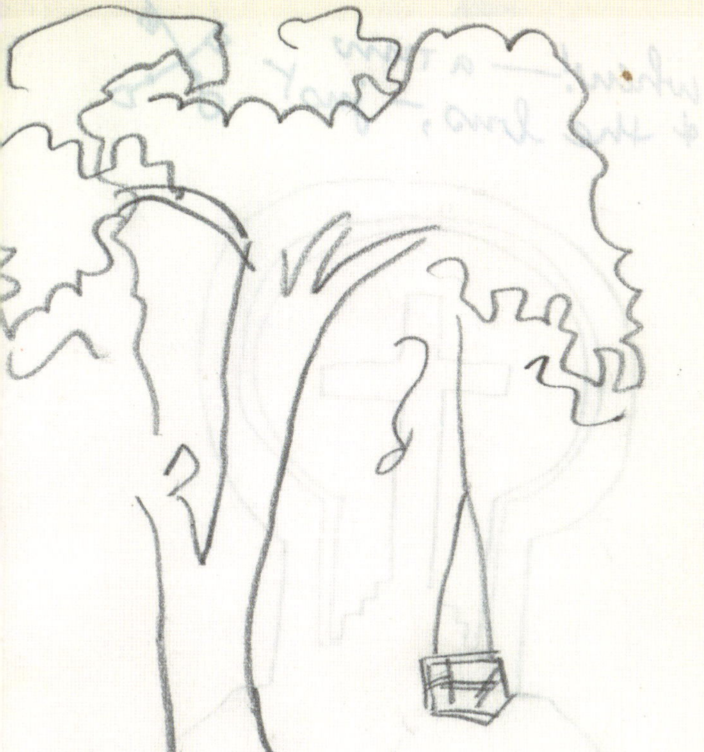

opened a conker
as white as a virgin

a rush for the bus

23rd / St George Tombland
St John Timberhill

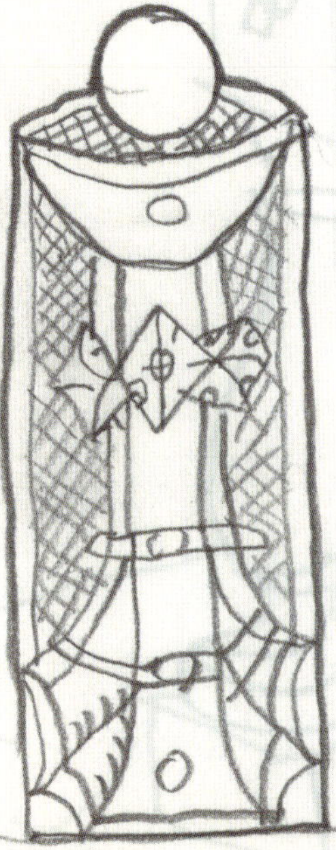

North Walsham S. Nicholas
– by bus (4 a brass)

23rd

Shut-down railway lines
to nowhere in Norfolk
& goodbye to The Bell.
A look at North Walsham
with an 8d teapot
Why & when the tumble towers?

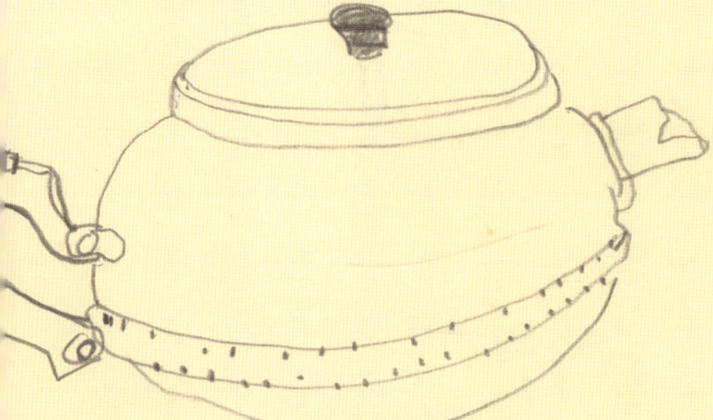

at The Towers
with Mrs Angell
– Mundesley on Sea
Two fillets plaice on Sea

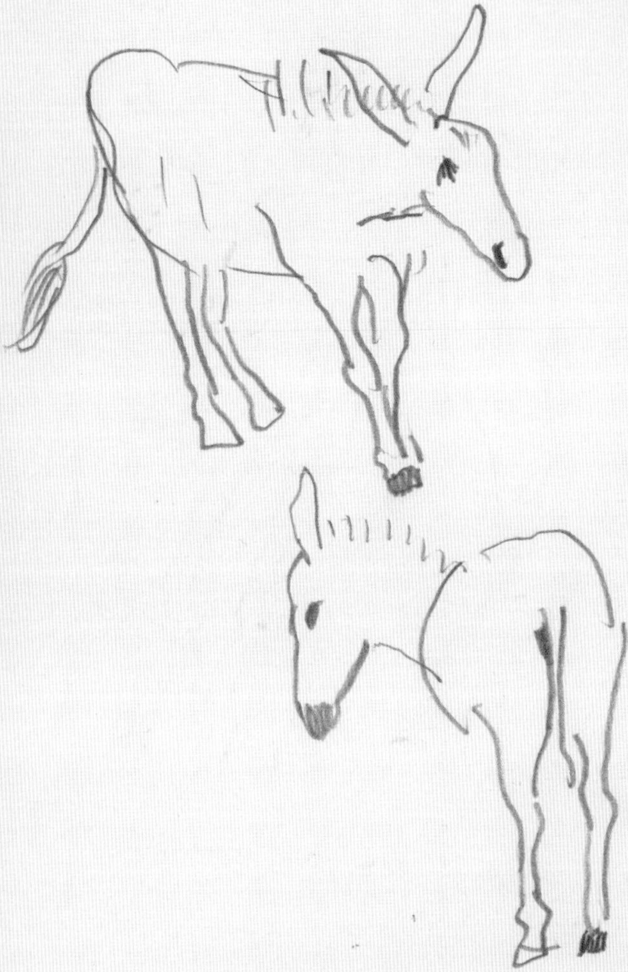

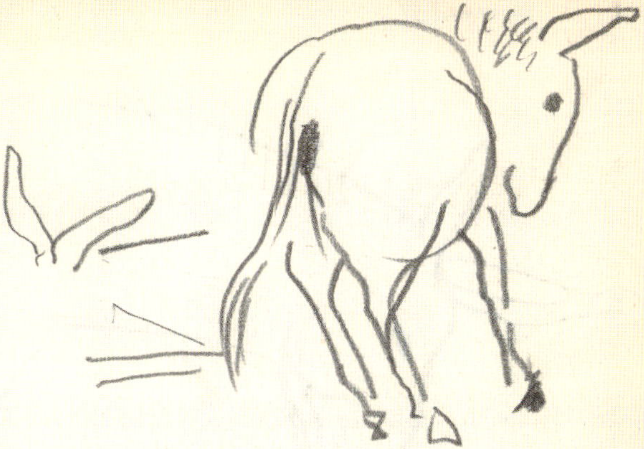

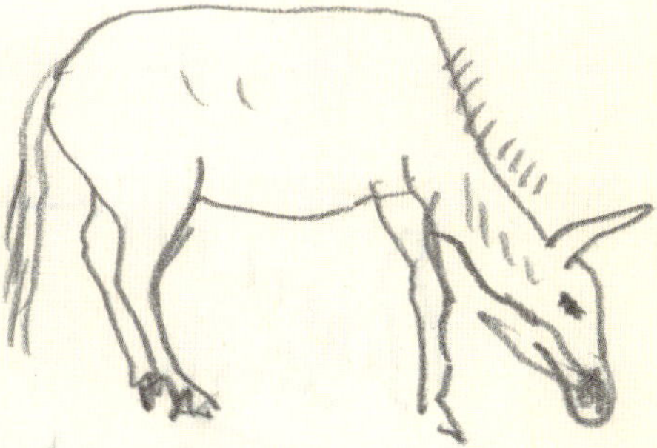

Saturday afternoon
with flies — ouch
& phoned N. Repns

Trinity XI

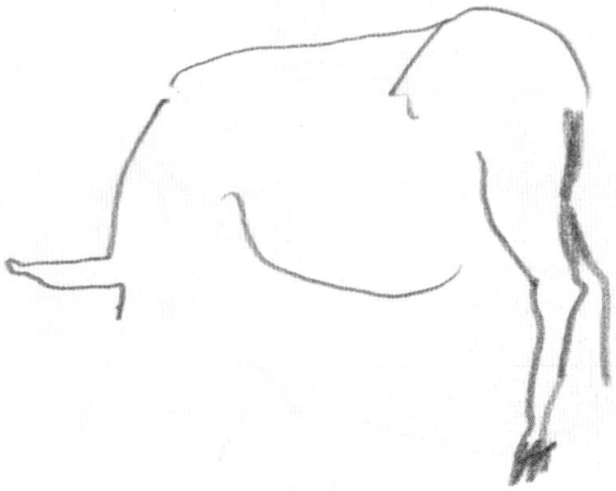

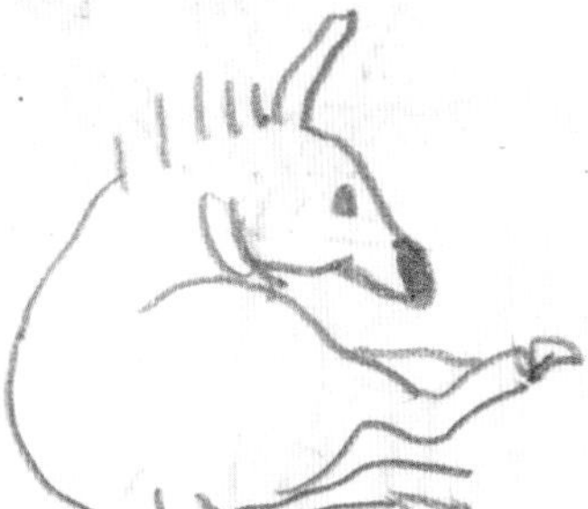

29 August

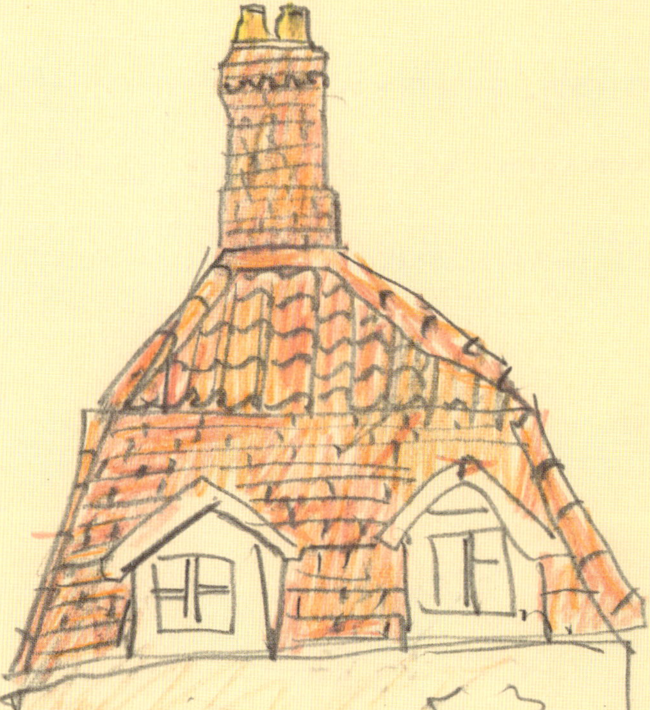

land of level crossings, au revoir

9th Sept

Quitted!

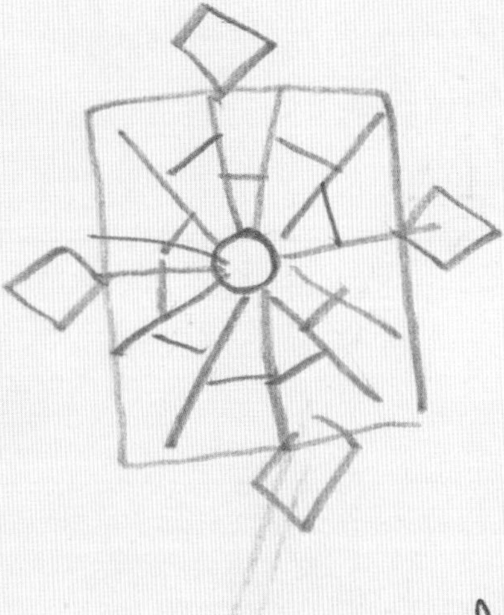

hedge bunny

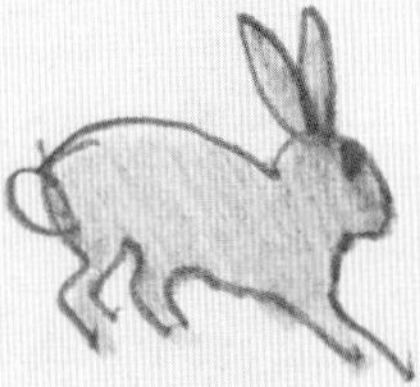

Modbury St Georges

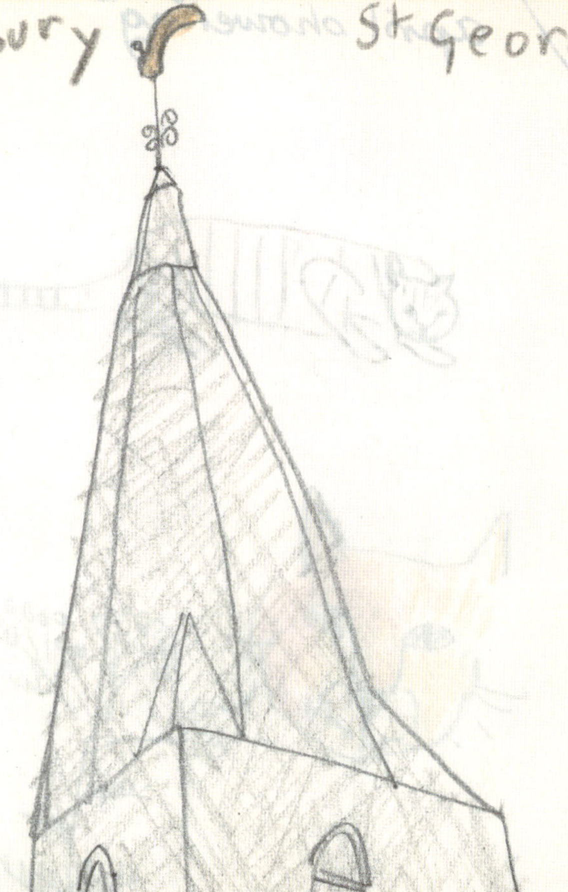

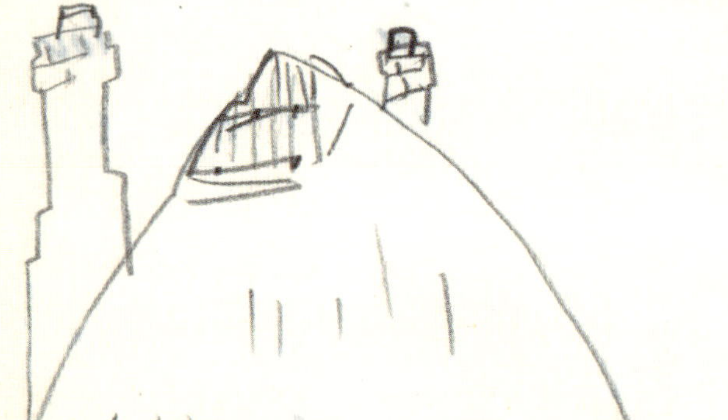

Hardy-like at Holbeton

28th
September

very misty - very early
& a cow wanting her calf
all night - noisy night.
7.30 Bus to the clang of churns
& waiting - milk train - wait.

NOTGNIDDAP
& Abbey Westminster

15.30 L'pool Street
to Essex eastish

18.17 Unknown Gunton
in the rain

Michaelmas

In a distant room
practising her pianoforte—
a little girl singing in a
Country rectory.

Sidestrand Evening Celebration
— & cake to celebrate St Michael

30th sept

One leaf in a large sky
& one wall of cowslip yellow

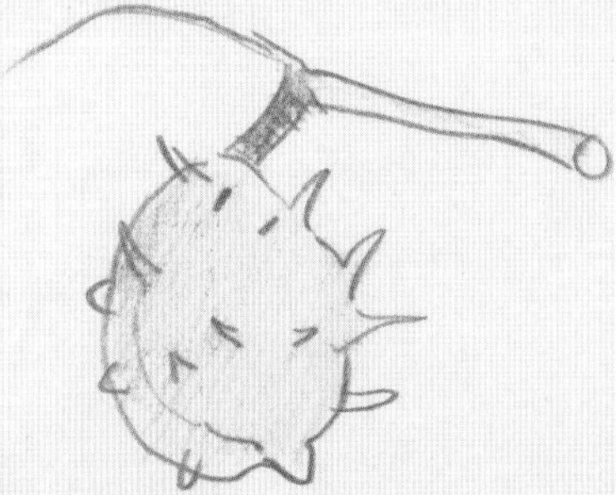

1st October

Jacktower - Jackdaws
+ still a Southrepps Martin
Cornshire –
Sugarbeetshire in
October - umber colours

Friday bathing whilst the hymns

2nd

Cromer in October
+ first octoberpheasant bangs

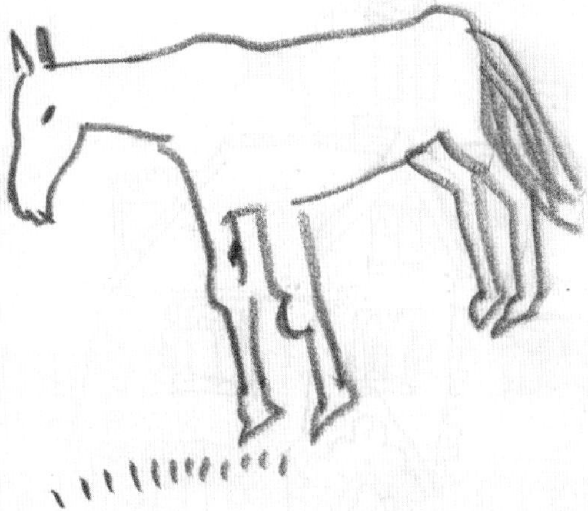

Trinity XVII

10th Oct

8.0 am at Northrepps with Susannah

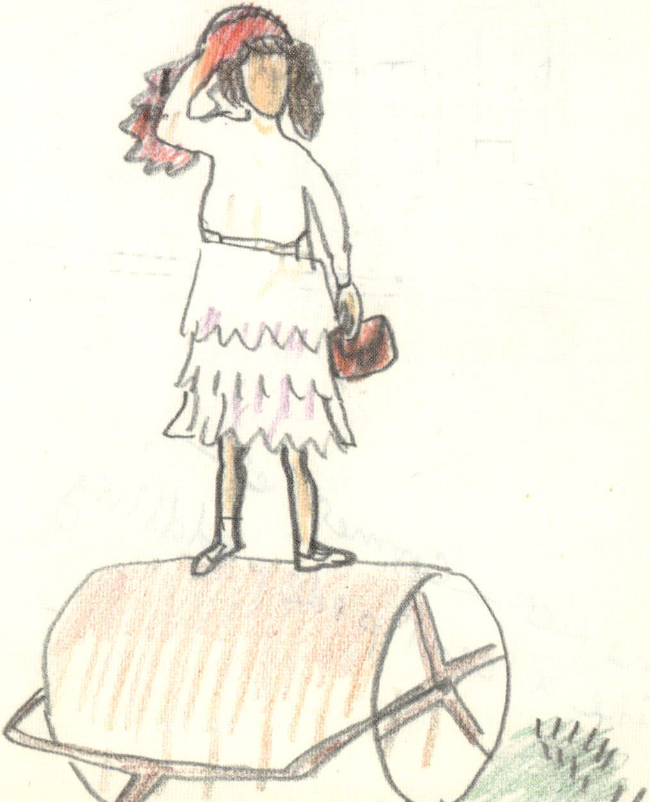

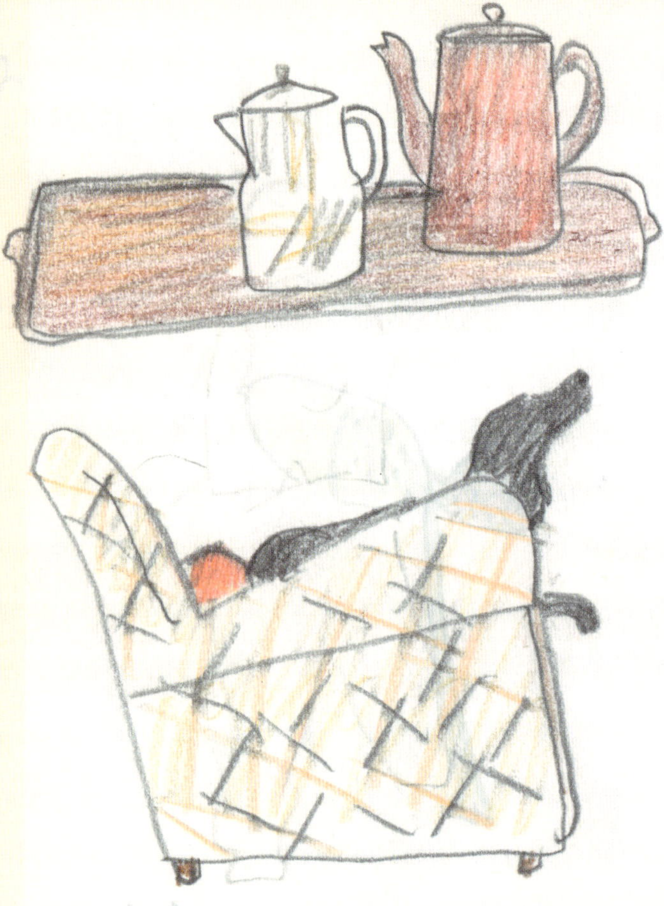

"We've got ten minutes" →

Trinity XX

— Sidestrand & Miss Blyth's.
Blowing, & the sea
seems nearer.
Talking of the
Hallelujah Indians

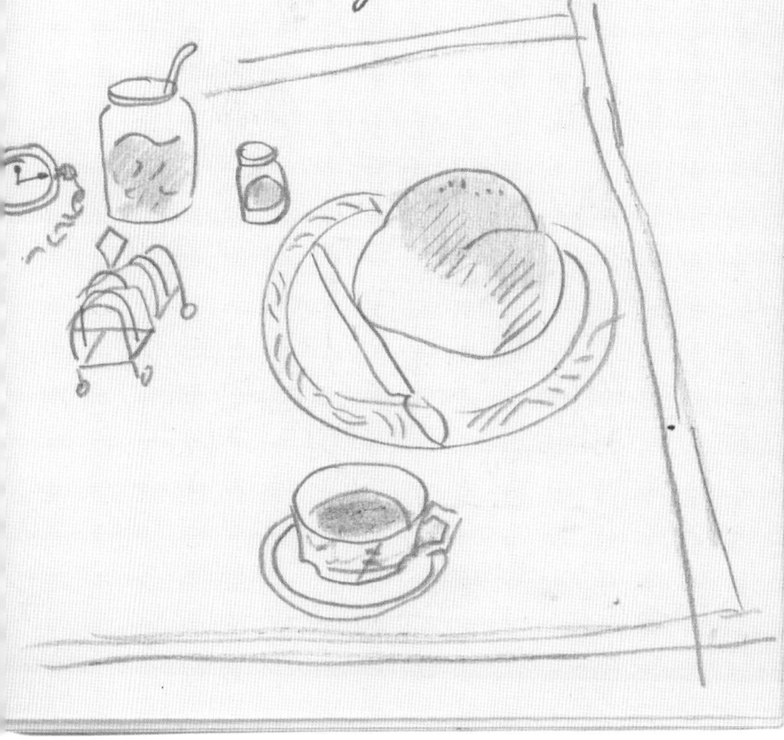

19th of Nov – & looks like it

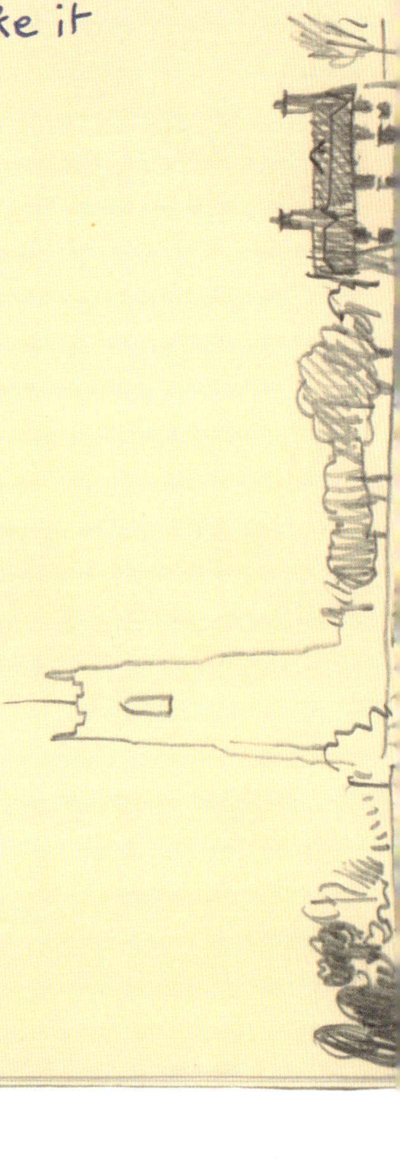

Next before Advent — 21st

– Colder, clearer

Susanna counting stars

– prickly, bright.

22nd

Coldly snowing

– door banging

white morning

– porridge weather

Banging-window wind — 25th

7th Dec.

Ruth: a moon
of egg
for breakfast
– hardboiled newmoon
& butter in a bowl

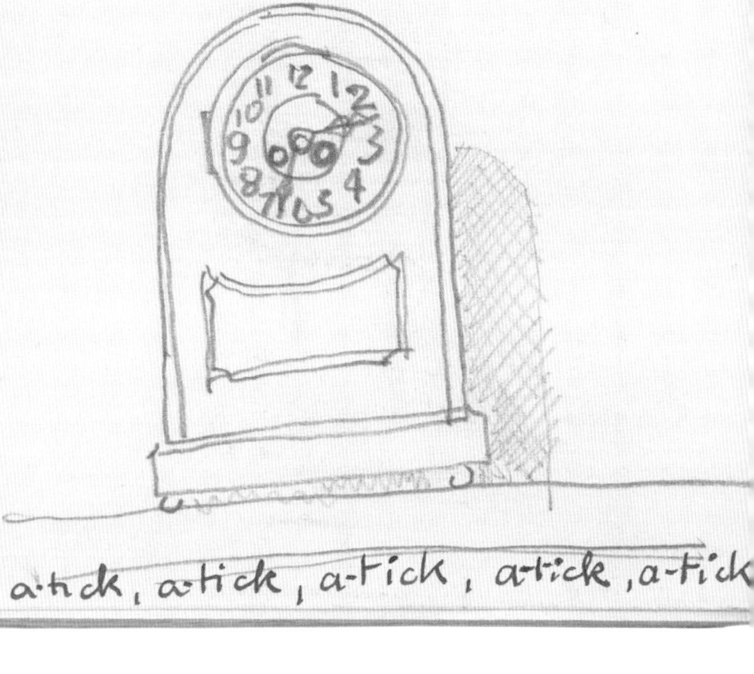

a-tick, a-tick, a-tick, a-tick, a-tick

Dining room –
& a-waiting room . . . . .
clerical case for books

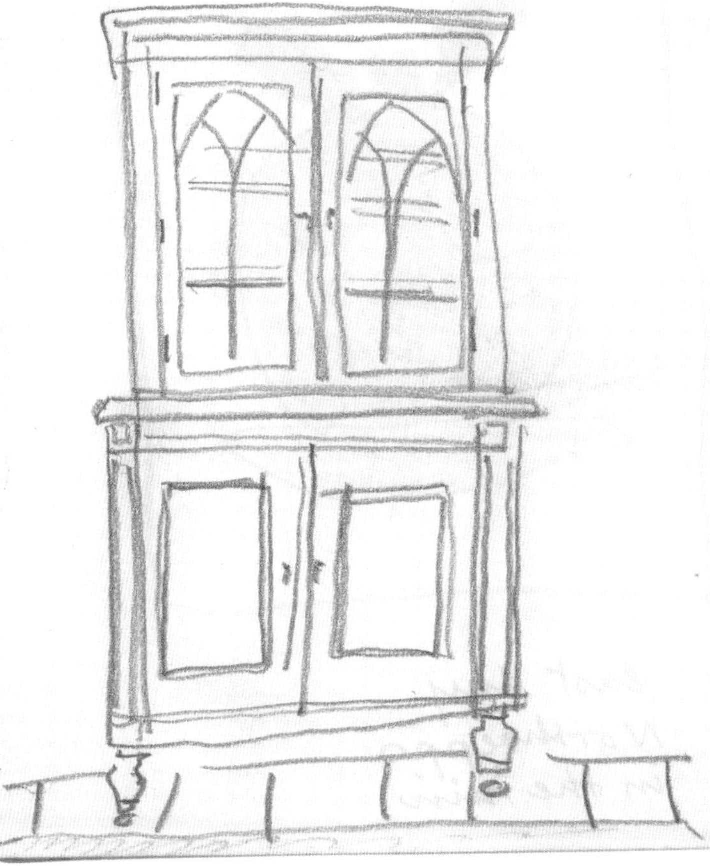

9th Dec.

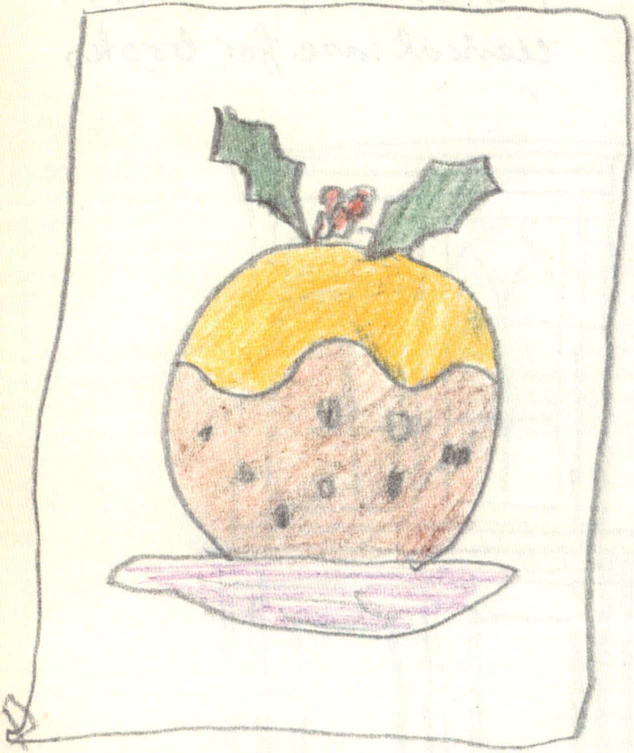

last day
Northrepps
in the rain

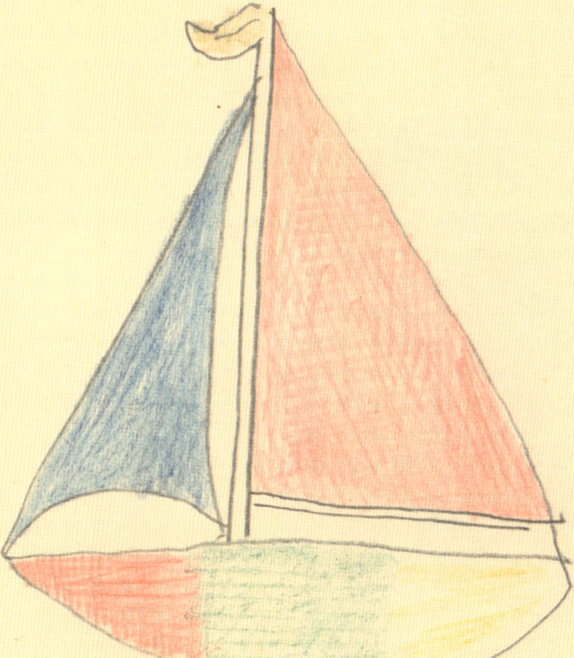

Dec 11th

E. at 7.45am
a spring of a day
– skied blue

again
in my nook
"The 'Ermitage"

12th

Advent III

geese haggling
"Dirty again"
Shake hands with Mr Prowse,
"Back for good?"
But good to be back.
how does
my garden grow?

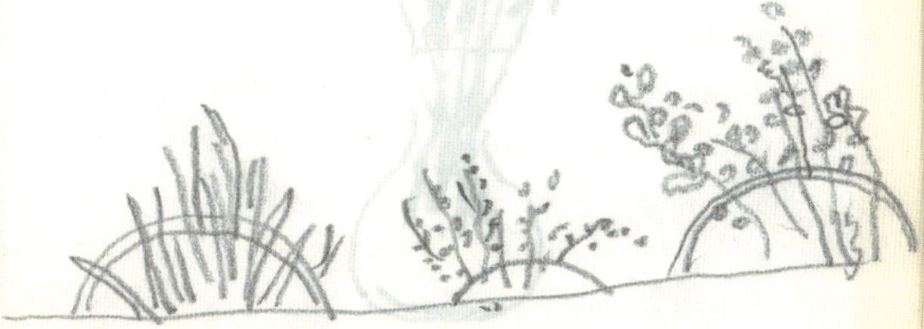

20th DEC

Sun on sea –
Dawlish brightwards
From the far East
& the warm west
to the –

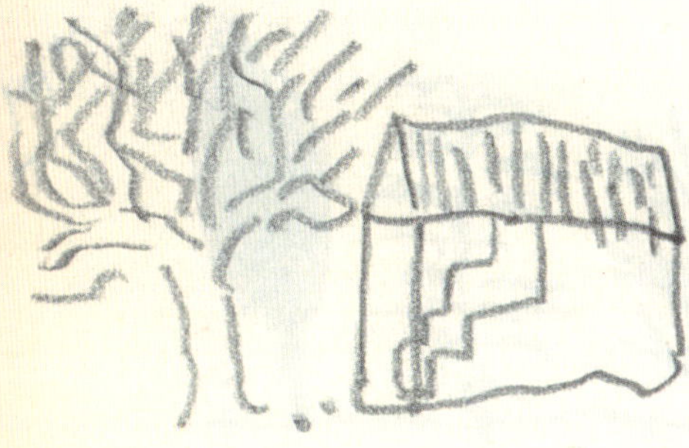

mellow in the evening

A puddle-paddle landscape
– cows at sea

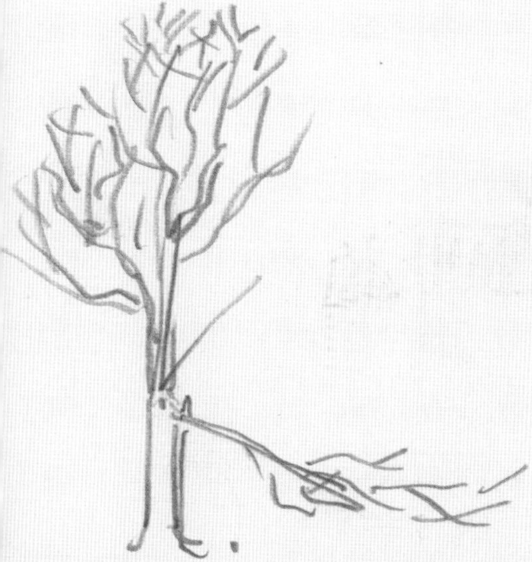

a wind in the night

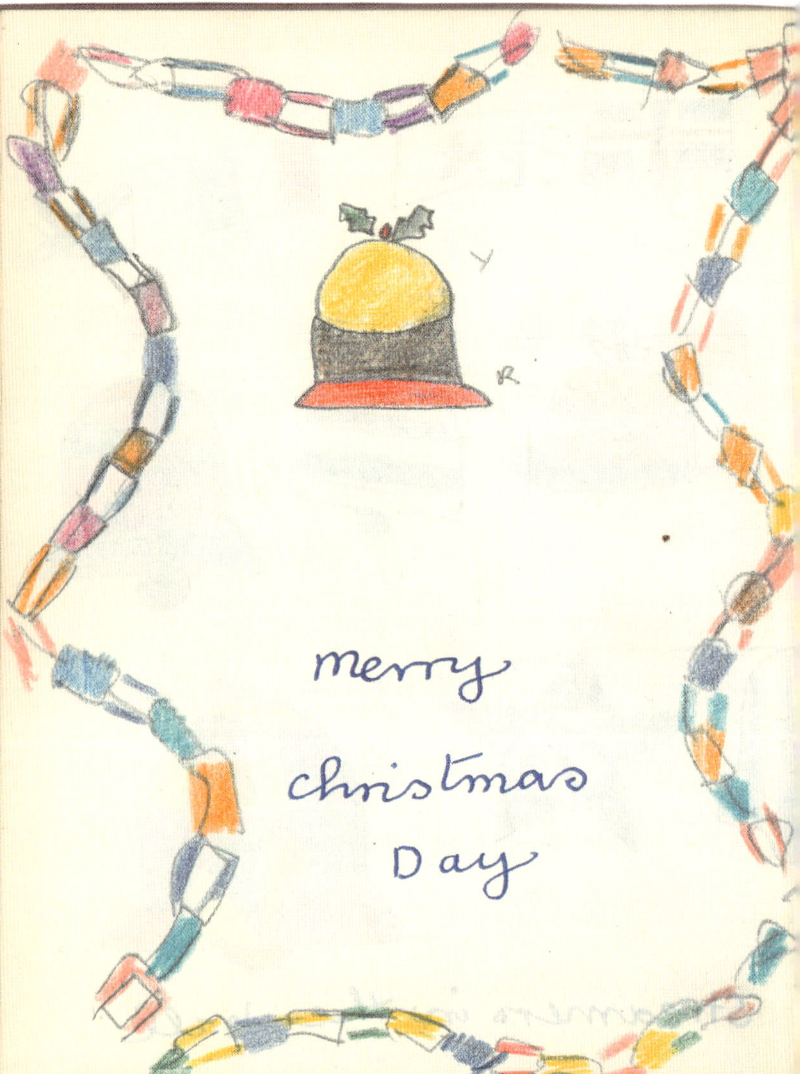
merry
Christmas
Day

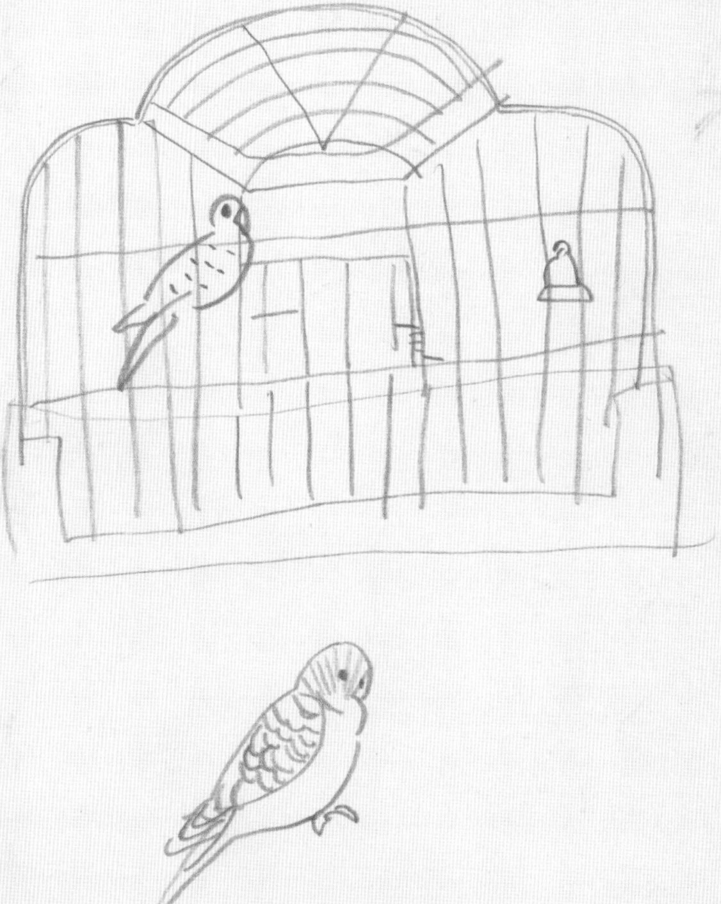